WIN/
WIN
SOLUTIONS

RESOLVING CONFLICT
ON THE JOB

WIN/
WIN
SOLUTIONS

Thomas J. Stevenin, Ph.D.

NORTHFIELD PUBLISHING
CHICAGO

ISBN: 1-881273-70-9

1 3 5 7 9 10 8 6 4 2

Printed in the United States of America

To Barbara,
my wife and best friend for three decades

In Tribute

Along with his family and others whose lives he had touched, I experienced a loss when I learned of Tom Stevenin's death earlier this year. But my sadness was quickly replaced by the richness of his memory and the quality of his ideas. One only needed to have a brief encounter with Tom or read his work to be optimistic about this journey we call life.

I knew Tom well and benefited greatly working alongside him as we introduced the PRIDE program he developed at Missouri Public Service. We often shared our views about the importance of people and their spirit in effective organizations. Tom was a man of conviction, with a strong faith and values rooted in biblical truths.

The demands and accelerating pace of modern enterprise seem almost always to be seeking something new—some new gimmick or fad or "spin" that might represent a breakthrough in achieving quality, consistency, and success. Tom would have none of it. He was a teacher, and the guidance he offered was built on a foundation of simple, yet honest affirmations, recognition of people and the power of positive reinforcement.

The PRIDE program he developed touched the work and personal lives of thousands. The results we experienced at Missouri Public Service were undisputed not only monetarily but in terms of the self worth which grew within all of us as a benefit of Tom's mentorship. And so, I was honored when Tom's wife, Barbara, asked me to write a tribute for this book—his last. But, in a way, it isn't his last. Tom's ideas live on in the minds and hearts of thousands who had the opportunity to read, listen, reflect, discuss, and learn with him.

ROBERT K. GREEN
President, UtiliCorp United
Kansas City, Missouri
May, 1997

CONTENTS

ACKNOWLEDGMENTS

Special thanks to Lori Carter for her careful, professional preparation of this manuscript. Lori works by the highest standards and is an excellent proofreader as well. Her numerous suggestions were also extremely valuable in terms of design, layout, emphasis, and content. Her coordination and assistance is greatly appreciated.

Special acknowledgments are also in order for Michael Ashcraft, Ami Johnson, and Spencer Warren, who reviewed and updated my previous training manuals. They helped this material come alive and fit the needs and format of this book. Their diligence and creativity are greatly appreciated. The strengths are theirs; the weaknesses are mine.

Thanks also to Dean Merrill for his final editing on behalf of Northfield Publishing.

In addition, I wish to acknowledge the many colleagues and mentors who have contributed to my professional development and my growing understanding of leadership and conflict resolution.

As one grows and matures in management and leadership, one inevitably learns from mentors. I am grateful for all I learned in my seventeen years with a large corporation, which went from $300 million in sales to well over $6 billion with only one major acquisition. This doesn't happen by accident.

I especially want to salute the valuable instruction of James Thomsen, F. Alton Erickson, Del Miller, and Robert E. Johanson.

Although they never supervised me directly, I've always appreciated the interest shown by Harold Hamil, Ernest Lindsey, and Harry Cleberg.

I'm especially grateful for the influence of Ernest Lindsey, the second president of Farmland, who taught me (and hundreds of others) that it was possible to be both an effective executive and a Christian gentleman.

Thanks also to Frank Weyforth, president and CEO of Marketing Resources of America, who demonstrated to me the effort it takes to go the second and third mile to satisfy the customer. I learned this valuable lesson better in a small business than a large one, and it was important to my growth and development.

INTRODUCTION

Sometimes, no matter how hard you try to leave your business problems at work, they follow you home. Or anywhere else you happen to go.

I will never forget the Sunday morning when the church usher tapped me on the shoulder near the end of the service. I had known him a long time. I grew up with his son.

"There's kind of a wild-looking man downstairs. He wants to see you. Would you like some help?"

"Yes," I said, "as soon as possible."

While my friend Bill Kahl went for help, I tiptoed downstairs to have a look. I saw the problem immediately.

Our company had a program to hire, train, and place ex-convicts (hopefully not for management positions) and Vietnam veterans. Most of these people made very good employees and sincerely appreciated the opportunity. This man had been an exception. Three times in the last thirty days he had gotten into fights in our battery plant in North Kansas City, Missouri, which was already a dangerous place to work.

So, we had released him. Despite the obvious evidence of his misconduct, he was claiming discrimination and had come to get the man he thought responsible for his dismissal—me.

As I approached the building's lower hall, he covered up what seemed to be (and later turned out to be) a revolver in his back pocket. This was my first real lesson in the fact that personnel conflict can get messy.

Fortunately, help arrived about that time in the person of Bill and the nearby police. They helped usher him on his way.

Before he left, I told him I still wanted to help him. I promised that if he would complete certain programs and get on top of his emotional problems, he could call me back, and we'd help him find a position he could handle.

He was in great emotional chaos, but he still wanted to succeed. I'll never forget his parting words: "I'll follow through on all that. And I will get a job. In fact, if I don't, may God strike me dead."

That must have been what happened, because I never saw him again.

Fortunately, not all organizational conflicts are this combustible. Some you just spend the rest of your life shaking your head over.

Like the time I got to help a junior personnel officer in a packing plant separate two women fighting on the floor of the entrails room. Due to a sudden shift change, they had discovered they were both living with the same man. I'm not sure whether I did them a service or not. I do know that somehow the organization got involved in their lives in a way it had never intended to nor wanted to.

Then, I'll always remember the one that made me mad.

That was the rather arrogant man who walked into my office one day and claimed I was forcing him to "live in sin."

Even though I've made more than my share of errors in supervising employees, I found this implication a bit of a stretch. I controlled my resentment long enough to ask how so.

He pointed the finger at our company policy at that time (since abolished) that people could not continue to work in the same department if they married each other. It simply created too many supervisory problems. Hence, from this man's standpoint, he and his girlfriend had no choice but to "live in sin."

I was never sure, from the company's point of view, what the right position was on this policy. But I do remember the happy day six months later when he astonished me by poking his head in the door and endorsing the policy he had once criticized. It had saved him from making "the biggest mistake of my life," he claimed.

These are the kinds of individual, daily, personal conflicts that managers live with day to day. On top of these are the larger conflicts that rage between powerful administrations with different goals and agendas. You cannot be an effective leader today unless you are prepared to deal with these.

That's what this book is all about. It is based on a lifetime of experience in corporate and organizational life. In that time, I've seen *good* conflict actually bring improvement to organizational life and decision making. In other instances (too many), I've seen *bad* conflict do great damage to programs and persons. I've become increasingly keen to find out what makes the difference.

I believe our ability as leaders to produce positive outcomes from conflict depends on the following:

- Our understanding of certain sick, obtuse personalities
- Our understanding of anger and how it fits in with conflict
- Our ability to master certain leadership techniques (such as confrontation)
- Our care in preparing people for change
- Our skill in emphasizing teamwork vs. internal competition
- Our creativity in designing recognition and rewards
- Our capacity to see beyond positions, power, and politics— to see persons of great worth despite their faults and foibles

This is a book for leaders. You will get the most from it if you are a leader, aspire to be one, or want to be a much better one.

You will notice that I sometimes cross over from the corporate world to use illustrations from the church world. That's because I am a citizen of two kingdoms. I'm endlessly fascinated by the fast-changing world of business; I love it and can't learn enough about it! But my other passion is the church. More than anything else, I would love to strengthen it and make it even more effective than it is after two thousand years.

The two worlds have much to teach each other. Their new willingness to learn from each other is one of the most exciting things I've lived to see. In fact, to have played a very small part in bridging this gap has been my highest joy in recent years.

—THOMAS J. STEVENIN, Ph.D.
Kansas City, Missouri

PART ONE

WHAT A MENAGERIE

C H A P T E R   O N E

THE SHERMAN TANKS

A leader friend of mine says there are basically three kinds of people in most circles of relationships:

1. *People who give us energy.* These people reinvigorate our exhaustion with new enthusiasm and ideas. They are not easily offended; they always go the extra mile. They are not pushovers or pleasers. They are strong people with strong convictions tempered by an inner spirit of caring and compassion.

They do not demonize their opponents in the coarse style of political and public dialogue that has become so popular today. They may disagree with others, but they never lose sight of the person behind the position.

2. *People who maintain our energy.* These are coworkers and team members who give equal to what they take from us. They require feedback and leadership, but they also provide good feedback, affirmation, and positive reinforcement. They understand that their first task is to play their own position on the team; their second task is to help you play yours. These people are genuine colleagues. We look forward to being with them at work.

3. *People who drain our energy.* When you look up and see this person coming across the room, you instinctively say to yourself, *Uh-oh, trouble is on the way.*

You may not know what shape the trouble will take, but you are absolutely certain it will occur. Why? Because it always does.

These are the people who drain us emotionally. Each time they arrive on our doorstep they come with a problem—never a solution. If there is no problem, they create one. I love the old story of the knight who rode into the king's palace, where the following conversation took place:

> *King:* "Knight, where have you been?"
> *Knight:* "I've been pillaging and ravaging your enemies on the eastern front."
> *King:* "But, I don't have any enemies on the eastern front!"
> *Knight:* "Well, King, you do now!"

I've spent most of my adult life counseling and consulting with executives and leaders of all types of organizations. Invariably, when I find a leader who is burned out, exhausted, or depressed, he or she is totally surrounded by draining relationships. The immediate staff is too weak. The leader is propping up everyone else. He's nurturing everyone; no one is nurturing him.

This kind of person simply must find colleagues who can replenish energy.

On the road of leadership, you will no doubt run into scores of people who drain you. Some of them actually mean no harm. It's just that major change takes its toll on these people. They have great difficulty making their way through new surroundings, procedures, and relationships. They are incredibly passive when it comes to the enterprise's success or failure. Most of them cave in, slip up, and slide around, despite their best efforts to stay on course.

They are hard to spot. They operate by stealth. I call them the Stealthy Stalkers. More about them in the next chapter.

There are also human beings who purposely create hazards on the road to change. They will quite intentionally become speed bumps, if not roadblocks. It takes an inordinate amount of time and energy to navigate around and through them.

To use another transportation analogy, these people are not even trying to help the engine of change pick up steam. They are trying to derail the train.

After thirty years of organizational consulting, I am convinced some individuals will eventually blow up any program they are connected with. They repeat this pattern over and over again. I refer to these people as Sherman Tanks.

There is nothing subtle about them. They won't sneak up on your blind side. They're more likely to come right at you with guns blazing! They roll over people. They kill the spirit of a team. They rob an organization of its soul.

They may stop progress just to be noticed. They may react to a perceived or actual loss of personal control either at work or outside the workplace. Or they may simply not want to see any change enacted at all. At least not any changes they didn't totally engineer themselves. In other words, they might think change is OK their way, but not yours.

We might politely call these people "difficult," and impolitely call them any number of names. They are people you are not only bound to run into but have to go around, under, or over to get ahead. Even then, you may find yourself dragging them along behind you, kicking and screaming all the way.

In their own minds, they think they are helping. They don't see themselves as destroyers of teamwork. They see themselves as vital to the process. They sometimes even think they are saving the situation. They view themselves often, in my experience, as the tough-minded individuals who have to rescue all the other incompetents.

These types are easy to see but not easy to respond to. Here are the most obvious types:

THE DOMINANT DICTATOR

These are the self-proclaimed aristocracy of the "office palace." These despots simply and deeply believe their way is *the* way. They are often greatly wrong, but never in the slightest doubt!

Unfortunately, they don't lead so much as bully their way through the workaday world. They know what to do in every situation, and so, they have no need to hear the views of anyone else. They're not interested in seminars or workshops. Simple "truths" should be obvious to all those around them.

They believe their all-knowingness has been clearly established in some way. If not preordained by divine providence, it has been obtained by virtue of some previous business coup (bloodless or otherwise) or some past achievement. They will fight to maintain their perceived position by overpowering their opponents.

Conversations with Dominant Dictators are always one-sided. They will attempt to keep the focus on themselves by any means possible—outright filibuster, if need be, so that no one can get a word (let alone a complete thought) in edgewise.

Should someone miraculously manage to make a point, no matter how worthy, a Dominant Dictator will rarely, if ever, give in to it. He will fight back with every fiber of his being, without any regard for the thoughts or feelings of others.

Marshall Shelley says:

> This kind of person is a steamroller who flattens anyone in his way with his overwhelming certainty that his is the only way to do it. Negotiation is a dirty word; compromise unspeakable. If this person is on a board that has settled a sensitive issue privately, but he wasn't completely satisfied with the decision, he's likely to bring it up again in a meeting because he enjoys the fireworks.[1]

One of the saddest examples I ever knew was a man who had an obsession with being great. He so desperately wanted to be somebody. He hated the reality of being a nobody. He was passed over for promotion at the plant. Then he ran for an office in the union and was totally rejected by the members.

In desperation, he tried to take over a small rural church. He was there every time the doors were opened. He volunteered for everything. He became indispensable. But his motives were all wrong. There was no joy in what he did. He was using the church to satisfy his deep craving to be somebody. Each act of service was an opportunity to tighten his control over the organization. The church almost died in his death grip. He later repeated this pattern in several other churches. Each failure left him in deeper bitterness.

One mystery is why so many people are willing to be dominated by despots. Why do people willingly serve and even die for such unattractive figures as Jim Jones or David Koresh? One expert suggests five reasons:

> *They are afraid.* For a complex series of reasons, their innate fear keeps them from standing up to the person controlling them. It

can be fear rooted in the past, or perhaps the person controlling them is bigger, more fierce, more powerful, or has authority over them, like a parent. For whatever reasons, fear holds them back from taking deliberate steps to deal with the oppression.

They are angry. They don't know how to deal with their anger, so they do nothing, thinking benign responses are better than the requirements of bitter confrontation.

They are ashamed. The regrets are stacked so high in their hearts that they assume there are no alternatives. Their shame draws their view of themselves so low that they feel unworthy and unfit to be standing in judgment of someone else.

They are in bondage. Their lives are a series of unfortunate choices that have obliterated their resolve. Little spirit or spunk is left— just a disappointment that gnaws away at their confidence. They are convinced that nothing they could do or say would make any difference, so they resign themselves to a life of being coerced and manipulated.

Passivity comes naturally to them. What they do better than any-thing else is roll with the punches. They're gifted at adaptability and know they're outgunned in a verbal duel, so they don't even try.[2]

THE CONTROL FANATIC

This person differs from the Dominant Dictator only in the level of perceived omniscience. Control Fanatics don't profess to have all the answers; they just want to have all the control over their implementation. These are the kind of persons who would rather get lost than get directions.

They want to sign and send out all marching orders. And they want all parties to report directly back to them and them alone.

Actually, for these people control is more than something they want. It is something they crave, emotionally. The compul-sive need to control their surroundings and situations often takes on the dynamics of an addiction.

Dr. Gerald Piaget defines a controlling person as "someone who consistently controls too much or at the wrong times— someone who needs to be in charge, who can't let go. In other words, someone who can't hold with an open hand when it is necessary or preferable to do so."[3]

Perhaps the clearest mental image of the consummate Con-trol Fanatic can be found at a nearby preschool or day care center. I'm talking about toddlers. Toddlers are little people working so hard to be in control of their environment that their efforts can be downright comical. It is fascinating to see the different ways they attempt to assert their control: temper tantrums, fits of anger, pouting spells, silent treatments.

They attempt to act like they're in charge, no matter how painfully clear it is to everyone around them that they are not. I remember an occasion when our family was ready to leave for some Saturday errands. Our three-year-old decided he didn't want to go. With great authority he stood in the front door of the house with arms and legs spread wide, blocking the entrance. "No way," he announced to two grown adults . . . who quickly picked him up and put him in the car.

Such behavior is understandable in a small child trying to find his identity in the world. In mature adults, it's very sad.

While Control Fanatics may bully or intimidate like Dominant Dictators, they are just as likely to pout their way through the process of change. Like toddlers, they achieve their goals equally well through sulking or tantrums, or just by worrying the situation to death. They even enjoy being perceived as depressed. They love having the whole group "concerned" about them. They manipulate the emotions of sincere, caring people who often have difficulty interpreting their behavior correctly.

In another form, the Control Fanatic controls by being overbearing. Like a gnat constantly hovering above the workers, nagging them onward, incessantly buzzing about their ears, the person is more of an annoyance and distraction than a leader helping a team achieve a goal.

Here are some reasons why all leaders should resist the drive to overcontrol employees or family:

- Regardless of how wise or well-meaning our control may be, the other person has an innate need to be in control of himself. Therefore, he will resist even the most loving suggestions.
- The person we try to control will find it difficult to trust us. Therefore, he will also be reluctant to confide in us.
- We could end up resenting the people we're controlling, because they have become so dependent on us that they're now a burden.

- Ultimately, control will erode our ability to enjoy genuine intimacy within our closest relationships. For married couples, high control can destroy the ability to relate to each other in healthy and happy ways.
- High control destroys the free exchange of confidence and loyalty between parents and children.
- Controlling others' lives can exact a high price physically. The stress of controlling others can make us sick.

The sad reality is that the controller often does not have the skills to match his/her enormous need to micromanage. Therefore, associates not only chafe under the constant supervision, but they also grow disillusioned as things become more and more of a mess. In the end employees begin hiding issues, making secret decisions, and leaving the controller out of the loop —which, ironically, is what the controller wanted most to avoid.

Religious organizations are not immune from this type of sick, unhealthy need to control. One writer says:

> I seldom have to go very far with a church before I find someone bending one of the sheep's legs behind its back and making it scream "uncle." Sometimes the man handling the lamb is wearing a clerical collar. But it cuts both ways, and sometimes the one crying "uncle" is not a sheep but a shepherd. The list of pastors who have been the main course at the deacons' feeding frenzy is endless.[4]

There's nothing wrong with power. There's nothing wrong with having a strong personality. In fact, one of the things missing in our culture today is strong, ethical leadership—especially in our homes. We long for a generation of leaders who don't lick their fingers and hold them to the wind when you ask what they believe. The issues that plague us cry out for people who make decisions from a position of power and strength rather than from the depth of insecurity.

But what happens when strength steps over the line? When it abuses its privileges and punishes with power? Many cultural things (crowded schedules, redefined roles, information overload) undermine relationships today. Their negative influence can be minimal, however, compared to the overwhelming damage done by high-control individuals wielding authority over others' spirits.

Jesus Christ himself warned his leadership team not to adapt this model.

> You know that the rulers of the Gentiles lord it over them, and their great men exercise authority over them. It is not so among you, but whoever wishes to become great among you shall be your servant, and whoever wishes to be first among you shall be your slave; just as the Son of Man did not come to be served, but to serve, and to give His life a ransom for many.[5]

Along the same lines He said, "But the greatest among you shall be your servant. And whoever exalts himself shall be humbled; and whoever humbles himself shall be exalted".[6]

Dr. Piaget provides this warning:

> Actually, most of us can turn into control freaks under the right circumstances. Some of us hide it better than others, and others use tactics which are so passive, indirect or elegantly subtle that they aren't recognized for what they are. But, at one time or another, almost all of us have let our control needs get the better of us.[7]

MR. ALWAYS RIGHT

This individual may not want to be in control of the situation, or to be the leader, nor even necessarily to have a particular thing done his way. He just wants to be right about everything he ever says, every point in an argument, every answer or opinion expressed about anything . . . or about nothing at all.

And if you don't happen to see the virtue of his position at first blush, he will unblushingly give you extra time to come around. One of his favorite expressions is "I'm sure if you really think about it, you'll agree with me." Makes your blood boil just to read that, doesn't it? Piaget gives an excellent description of this person:

> Placing themselves at the center of the universe, they have such a strong sense of their own self-importance and superiority that they act as if they have a right to call the shots in any and all situ-

ations. *No one can understand and handle things as well as I can,* they think—and believe that their businesses, families and possibly civilization itself would cease to exist if they were not available to give unsolicited advice, deliver lectures on proper conduct and mete out punishment for various misdeeds.[8]

It's no picnic having to listen to Mr. Always Right. And if you're within earshot, you'll be forced to listen, no matter which way the wind blows. If a project wildly succeeds, he'll be right there to say, "I told you so." If a project outright fails, he'll be right there to say the same thing.

Bucking human nature to the maximum, these are people who are making no joke when they say, "I thought I was wrong once, but I was mistaken." And believe me, they will repeat that hackneyed one-liner at some point, fully expecting you to think it's true this one time.

The one thing Mr. Always Right will never say is "I'm sorry."

The leadership tragedy of Richard Nixon is instructive. The former president went to his death without offering a clear apology for his misdeeds. Contrast this with President Reagan's Iran-Contra scandal (where far more laws were actually broken). Within twenty-four hours he apologized to the nation and promised it would never happen again. Although the enormity of this scandal greatly weakened his effectiveness in the second term, it did not drive him from office. It's hard to stay angry with a leader who apologizes. After eight years on the national stage, Ronald Reagan retired with an 80 percent approval rating and the affection of the American people. He knew there is no such thing as a leader who is never wrong.

RAMBO

This perpetual firecracker manipulates work associates (and sometimes managers) with the constant threat of a temper tantrum. He discovered early on that most people prefer to avoid emotional confrontations. Even those coworkers who don't care about whether the firecracker explodes would prefer not to be involved in a shouting match. Thus the firecracker creates for himself or herself a comfortable work environment because people step aside, make allowances, and avoid the dragon's breath.

As leaders, we must draw the line at the office door regarding angry outbursts, much as we do with drugs or drinking on the job. Rambo must be counseled to understand that unmanageable anger is (1) completely inappropriate for work relations and (2) won't earn any special treatment. Outlining standards of self-control can reduce the outbursts. If no improvement occurs, the person should be required to seek outside professional help.

If there is still no improvement, release Rambo. He is dangerous to other workers and a threat to you. If you don't think so, read your newspaper more carefully. Violence in the workplace is becoming a major problem.

Those who struggle with anger and temper control are sometimes the managers themselves. I once heard Lee Iacocca speak to the American Society for Quality and Participation. He admitted having to face up to his own inclinations toward fury in his career: "I was full of anger, and I had a simple choice: I could turn that anger against myself, with disastrous results. Or I could take some of that energy and try to do something productive. . . . It's always best to plow your anger and your energy into something productive."

Undeniably, managing others through anger does seem to work in the short-term. Difficult employees learn to stay out of the angry manager's way. Everyone is "good" when the boss is watching.

But Rambo doesn't manage others well for long. Consider three inevitable results of relating to others through anger:

1. *Rambo burns out.* Physically and emotionally, managers break down when, day in and day out, they attempt to manage by means of blood pressure and Maalox. Today's outburst has to be repeated tomorrow, with even more intensity, and employees come to expect an encore to the boss's fits of rage. The boss finds himself or herself always having to up the ante. What used to take only a harsh glance now requires a ten-minute tantrum.

2. *Good employees quit.* Bright, talented people don't stay long in the employ of perpetually angry managers. Recent analyses of exit interview data across industries show that good employees quit primarily because of interpersonal difficulties, not for financial reasons. One of the most common comments in exit interviews is "I just couldn't stand working for my boss."

3. *The best ideas are never heard.* An atmosphere of managerial

anger sends employees into a "safe mode"—that no-risk form of behavior in which only approved and traditional thoughts and actions are undertaken. After all, who wants to call down the wrath of Rambo?

As a consequence, angry managers find themselves more and more alone during the business day. Few employees ask for conferences or meetings. Left to themselves, angry managers find more time to brood and to pick new locations for lightning to strike.

THE NEGAHOLIC

Dr. No has the same old prescription for every new situation, namely, "Don't do anything I wouldn't do." And believe me, there isn't anything Dr. No wouldn't do to fix things so that nothing new ever happens. He is obsessed with fear and foreboding. He is totally risk adverse.

Our problem-centered news media play into this person's hands. The Negaholic sees little that is good; his negativism only grows as he reads news reports of air pollutants and contaminated fish. He grows leery and confused as one study tells him better health requires he avoid caffeine but a later study warns that decaffeinated coffee can boost his cholesterol level.

The Negaholic is a person who has seen a lot of changes in his lifetime, and was opposed to every one of them. If he or she can't talk you back into the same old way of doing things, they'll sure try to talk you out of doing anything new.

Whatever the thrust of any new initiative, Dr. No is right there to parry. According to Dr. No, no matter what it is:

• "It'll never work."
• "It'll never work here."
• "It'll cost too much money."
• "It'll take too much time."
• "It'll confuse too many people."
• "It'll involve too many people."
• "It'll be too radical a change."
• "It'll be too big of a headache to implement."
• "It'll be a wasted effort."

In essence—and this is the main concern—if we do what-ever's being suggested, "Things will never be the same again."

You've probably heard the old story of the elder in a church business meeting who was known for opposing everything. Someone proposed they purchase a new chandelier for the sanc-tuary. He responded: "I'm totally against it, and I'll give you three reasons: First, if we ordered it, no one would know how to spell it. Second, if it came, no one would know how to play it. And third, if we've got extra money, we need better lighting around here!"

The potential loss of comfort and certainty is enough to make those with negaholic personalities put up the fight of their lives against the very notion that change is necessary. In reality, change is not only necessary, it is inevitable. Nothing is more natural in life, nor more certain, nor more constant than change.

The types of persons who openly and actively deny this are not only an impediment to their own growth and improvement, but they all too often prove to be a drag on everyone around them. One expert gives ten symptoms of an organization too much in the control of negaholism:[9]

1. People's behavior is motivated out of a desire to protect themselves, each other, or to preserve the status quo rather than fulfill the mission of the organization.
2. People's individual compulsions, addictions, and neu-roses begin to dominate and determine the strategy, activities, and even the direction of the company.
3. Individuals turn the negativity they feel about them-selves toward the organization that employs them.
4. Employees spend the majority of their time criticizing or judging their coworkers, the management of the organi-zation, the policies, or the way things are being done instead of taking constructive action.
5. Employees act out the sentiment "Why would I want to be part of an organization that would have me as an employee?"
6. Individuals unconsciously work out their unresolved childhood issues (i.e., the pursuit of attention, recognition, approval, love, sibling rivalry, rebellion against authority figures, etc.) in a work environment.

7. The self-sabotage that individuals personally experience is transferred to the organization.
8. Dysfunctional behavior contaminates the employees, who in turn infect the customers, which seriously affects the bottom line.
9. The "I can'ts" have taken over through a long, slow process, inculcating the majority of employees in such a way that they have become addicted to their own negativity.
10. There is no consequence-management, and therefore, no incentive for individuals to strive for excellence and make a difference.

If leaders become cowed by these people and afraid to challenge them, they will lose spontaneity and creativity. Change is stifled, growth stunted, and the organization loses its creative edge.

THE SABOTEUR

This is the unhappy transfer employee, the demoted manager, the reassigned supervisor. They say little about their situation, but they implicitly invite everyone to watch them act out their anger against the company.

Those actions take many forms, including petty sabotage of company equipment or procedures, flagrant violations of basic policies, obvious lack of respect for leadership, and quiet mockery of other employees' motives and efforts. Saboteurs have decided to go down in flames, and want as large an audience as possible. Their reasons range from crude revenge to a subtle form of self-assertion. Saboteurs calculate that their downward course may reveal to other employees the underside of their professional lives. *They'll see I was right all along* is the implication.

This person is among the most dangerous of difficult people for the company, because he or she has nothing to lose. Given no hope of recognition or advancement, the Saboteur sees no reason not to throw a bug or two into a computer program, forget to pass along important messages, or abuse expense accounts and sick leave. Nor does the Saboteur try to stop other discontents in the company from following these leads.

Managers must act decisively to isolate and monitor the Saboteur. These malcontents have an almost cancerous influence on the attitudes of other workers. If termination is not an option, they should be placed in highly structured work environments where little long-term damage can be done to the company. Even then, watch their activities closely.

Although all these types of people are difficult to deal with, they are also the most obvious. They are not hard to notice. They would be hard not to notice.

There are also subtler, equally difficult types who are harder to identify. I call them the Stealthy Stalkers. They seize control before the leader even perceives the threat. We'll discuss some of them in the next chapter.

NOTES

1. Marshall Shelley, *Well-Intentioned Dragons: Ministering to Problem People in the Church* (Carol Stream, Ill.: Christianity Today, 1985), 39.
2. Tim Kimmel, *How to Deal With Powerful Personalities* (Colorado Springs: Focus on the Family, 1994), 202–203.
3. Gerald W. Piaget, *Control Freaks: Who They Are and How to Stop Them From Ruining Your Life* (New York: Doubleday, 1991), xi.
4. Kimmel, *Powerful Personalities*, 12.
5. Matthew 20:25b-28, New American Standard Bible.
6. Matthew 23:11-12, NASB.
7. Piaget, *Control Freaks*, xi.
8. Ibid., 5.
9. Cherie Carter-Scott, *The Corporate Negaholic* (New York: Ballantine, 1991), 4–5.

THE STEALTHY STALKERS

Don't look now, but some dangerous people may be gaining on you. To the leader, these employees may not seem problematic. They may have good personalities and even appear to be strong supporters. Yet everywhere they go, war seems to break out. Dead bodies are strewn along the road when they pass.

Here is a gallery of people who are difficult, yet hard to spot.

THE PASSIVE/AGGRESSIVE

Passive/aggressive people are very tough to figure out. Their particular paradox is not that they express themselves both passively and aggressively. It's that they express their aggression passively.

When angry, they are most likely to give you the silent treatment. They say nothing despite being directly questioned, cajoled, or otherwise prodded to make a response. Theirs is a loud silence.

It is relatively easy to see that these people are upset with something. Yet, the vacuum of response makes it very difficult to know why, what about, or in general, where they stand on any given issue or project. Their view is that if you really cared about them, you would already know what is bothering them. They are like the marriage partner who tells a spouse, "If you really loved me, you wouldn't have to ask what's wrong."

The silent treatment does not mean these individuals have nothing to say about the subject at hand. More often they have no skill at expressing anger in any socially acceptable fashion. Instead, they turn their anger inward to simmer into a dangerous stew.

They are nearly always depressed. Medical doctor Paul Meier states: "In reality, 95 percent of all cases of depression are caused by repressed anger toward an abuser or toward oneself. A majority of anxiety disorders involve a fear of becoming aware of our unconscious repressed anger toward our abusers or toward ourselves."[1]

The Passive/Aggressive is perpetually set for detonation. His fuse may be long, but once it's lit, you'd better run for cover. This person is an expert at getting even with those who have "wronged" him for any reason. He manipulates through intimidation, keeping those around him walking on eggshells.

Unlike the emotional extrovert (who blows up frequently but cools off quickly), the Passive/Aggressive builds anger to the point where it explodes in bizarre and incomprehensible ways. How often do we pick up the newspaper and read about a teenager who has gunned down a whole family? Inevitably, news reporters descend on the neighborhood to inquire about the young person and are told, "He was quiet, a model student, very polite, someone who never gave anyone any trouble." In reality this individual was a seething cauldron of resentment and anger. He just never learned to express that anger in a healthy way.

I urge leaders, managers, and teachers to draw out quiet persons who "never cause any trouble." It may, of course, just be their nature to be quiet. But it may also be that no one is really in touch with this child or adult. Meanwhile, a world of anger and violence is building inside.

THE ETERNAL EXTROVERT

Generally speaking, Eternal Extroverts are generally speaking. They are never quiet or reflective. Eternal Extroverts believe in free speech and plenty of it. They may expose their secrets and skeletons the first time you meet them, often within the first twenty minutes. They may go on talking hours longer. If you've supervised or worked with such a person for any length of time, you know everything about him. You know things you don't want to know.

You not only know all the children but feel you've partially raised them. These people have no private areas. They leave no space in a relationship. They overwhelm it. They smother it. Every relationship must become a personal friendship, or they feel they've been personally rejected.

This type of person talks in order to think. He says things he's never thought of before. He just thought of it the moment he verbalized it. He often does not mean what he says first and frequently modifies his own extreme positions. So don't leave the meeting early! The Eternal Extrovert may talk himself into or out of several positions before it's over.

These people are extremely engaging, often very entertaining, and very enjoyable. They are masters of small talk. They can talk almost endlessly about the smallest detail, or broad-stroke their way across a vast canvas of topics. They are never inhibited by their lack of factual information.

People with this personality type are often cast in the role of salespeople, and for seemingly good reason. Their uncanny ability to establish instant rapport with nearly everyone undoubtedly gets them in more doors than those who are less gregarious.

Unfortunately, once inside the door, Eternal Extroverts may get so wrapped up in telling their life story, or coaxing the life story out of somebody else, that they may forget why they knocked on the door to begin with.

Some firms are now making good salespeople out of introverted personalities. While their strength is not in schmoozing, they can make up for it simply by being good listeners and having the personal discipline to follow through on assigned tasks.

From a management standpoint, the same qualities that make extroverts endearing to customers make them hard to hold accountable. Remember, they want to make you feel good. They want to feed you what they think you want to hear. Unfortunately, they are much more likely to feed you baloney than to get to the meat of whatever issue is at stake.

THE MARTYR

The Martyr has an insatiable desire to be noticed. This individual deeply wants you to know how tremendously selfless and caring, overworked and neglected he or she is.

You can never win a game of one-upmanship with Martyrs. No matter how long you worked, they worked longer. No matter how little sleep you got last night, they slept less. No matter how much you help and give and care for the poor, the hungry, the huddled masses yearning to breathe free, they help, give, and care more than you do. And they not only want you to know it, but admire them for it.

The fact that Martyrs habitually exaggerate their efforts is not to say that they make no effort. They usually do in fact get a lot done. They just want to make sure you know about it. This may require them almost literally to lie down in front of you so you'll notice. And that's where they become speed bumps to progress.

The essential problem of Martyrs is low self-esteem. They do not have a sufficient sense of self-worth to be able to say no or assert their own boundaries. They endlessly seek to justify their existence by being the first to arrive, the last to leave, and the hardest working on the least pleasant task.

Here are some characteristics of people who suffer from low self-esteem:

- Pessimistic outlook on life
- Lack of social skills
- Extreme sensitivity to opinions of others
- Extremely self-conscious about appearance
- View others as competition
- Must prove something—inadequate feelings
- Inability to enjoy who they are—present life pushed aside
- Rehashing conversations—"What did she mean by that?"
- Critical of others
- Defensiveness—can't admit mistakes
- Tendency to develop clinging relationships
- Inability to accept praise
- Letting others walk on them

- Fear of being alone
- Fear of intimacy
- Dependence on material possessions
- Worry—belief that the worst will happen
- Inability to express deep emotions
- Perfectionist—obsessive
- Need to be in control

Martyrs desperately need praise but seem to reject it even when they receive it. Praising them is like pouring water through a sieve. There's never enough, and it never lasts. They need to learn that true humility is not thinking less of yourself, but thinking of yourself less.

THE STAMP COLLECTOR

The Stamp Collector seems nice enough on the surface. He calls little attention to himself and almost never engages in angry outbursts. In fact, if asked he would probably deny that there was anything bothering him at all. He may even try to tell himself that he shouldn't make an issue out of the latest insult or grievance. He must try to forget.

In fact, he doesn't forget. He has no intention of forgetting. He pastes a stamp in his memory book of wrongs. When the book gets full, he brings it out and shows it to you. You will be amazed at his detailed recitation of the evidence that you are a truly terrible manager. That last stamp may have been only a two-center, but it was the last stamp! Out comes the book so you can see for yourself the enormity of your offenses.

Unfortunately, many stamp collectors are managers themselves. Instead of immediately confronting an employee with unacceptable behavior, they save up incidents for the so-called annual performance review (a sadomasochistic ritual still preserved in many organizations). W. Edwards Deming, the premier business consultant of the twentieth century, sometimes joked that Japan's two greatest competitive advantages were the American annual performance review and the M.B.A. degree.

Managers must come to understand that motivation is a daily, weekly process. The team must huddle frequently to plan strategy and take corrective action. Celebrating improvement and giving thoughtful feedback are daily events in a quality organization, not an awkward, unnatural meeting at year's end. There has yet to be a study indicating that these events improve anything, least of all performance. In fact, this practice often encourages stamp collecting.

THE LONE RANGER

The opposite of the extrovert, the Lone Ranger is almost completely isolated in the company, but sounds forth nevertheless with a flood of memos ("I want to bring to your attention . . ."), phone calls ("I thought you should know that . . ."), and letters to the company newsletter ("Management has again deceived workers by . . ."). This difficult person speaks as if representing a large employee power block; in actual fact, he or she sits stewing alone in a small cubicle, contemplating where angry lightning should strike next.

Most others employed in the immediate vicinity of the Lone Ranger quickly learn to ignore his or her strange campaigns. But managers can find him both irritating and destructive, especially when he sends anonymous messages to senior corporate officers, government regulatory agencies, and public interest groups.

The Lone Ranger is looking for an audience. The more people in the company who ignore him, the more strident and daring he becomes. Much of the anger that motivates the Lone Ranger may come from his or her social isolation.

That anger can be defused by welcoming the Lone Ranger as a member of the team. He needs to be brought in from the prairie. Interpret the social isolation and anger of the Lone Ranger as a plea to be included in company life.

THE CHRONIC LIAR

The Chronic Liar has burned most of his or her bridges in the company and has relatively little credibility. What the liar does say is immediately discounted by others who know his or her deceiving ways. The liar can look you in the eye and tell you absolute fabrications without blinking.

The liar wants the rewards of doing everything right while in fact doing many things wrong. Therefore, he or she is willing to lie in an effort to preserve appearances. And sadly, the lies often work for years. Fellow employees, even when they discover they've been deceived, usually grumble in silence instead of confronting the liar. They may feel it's an exercise in frustration to try to pin the liar down to the truth. He or she would probably squirm out by offering another lie.

One of my saddest experiences was trying to counsel a leader who was a Chronic Liar. He was clever, devious, and manipulative. He destroyed his leadership, his personal life, and almost destroyed the organization. Yet he was so slick that some people today still think *he* was the victim.

Most of us don't realize how severe this person's problems can be. You see, the Chronic Liar lies to everyone, including himself—sometimes so convincingly that he comes to believe his own version of events.

Such persons are an incredible problem for police, judges, and juries. Right after committing a horrendous crime, they are calm and cool. They can commit mayhem and then make small talk at a party. They show no signs of guilt or remorse. When accused, they are outraged at the charges. In their own eyes *they* become the victim.

This sociopathic personality is little understood in our legal system or in our society at large. At one time the true sociopath was rare, but in this amoral, overly tolerant society, he is becoming all too common.

Liars usually self-destruct in professional life, but on the way down they cause untold damage to organizations and individuals. The small lies that "explain" a late lunch or missing supplies quickly turn into huge lies that spell lost customers and litigation for the company.

At heart, the Chronic Liar usually has an almost phobic fear of failure—and that provides a starting place for his or her reclamation. The majority of business ventures at all levels are failures or only partial successes, even in the most profitable companies. Letters written to win new clients fail more often than they succeed. Sales calls strike out more often than they score. For successful professionals, failure isn't something to be ashamed of. It's the daily test of one's courage and ingenuity.

As a leader, you must confront the liar with a glaring untruth. Be absolutely clear that you do not believe his version of events. Then lead the conversation to the topic of how to handle failure. Occasional failures, while undesirable, are inevitable in anyone's career. Individuals with integrity stand up to their failures and work to overcome them.

THE BLAMER

Like the liar, the Blamer has alienated virtually all of his or her social contacts in the company, and can't even claim the liar's creativity to add credence to what he or she says. The blamer is nothing if not predictable. Faced with any question regarding statements, actions, or responsibilities, the Blamer passes the ball to someone—anyone—within range.

"I didn't get the letter sent to Mr. Jones because my secretary forgot to type it yesterday." This is a lie, of course; the letter was never given to the secretary to type. But it's a particularly dangerous form of lie because it places blame on an innocent party. The Blamer has not only given up personal integrity but has also disregarded the reputations or welfare of others. If a secretary has to take a bum rap for "forgetting" a letter, the Blamer breathes a sigh of relief for getting off the hook one more time.

The Blamer with the accusing finger has found the most convenient way to excuse himself of all responsibility: Finger a foe, any foe. Fix the blame. Assign guilt. Lay the full responsibility at the other's doorstep. If the partner willingly grovels, the interaction is complete. Every Blamer seeks a placater; every guilty victim, a tyrant. It takes two to continue these cyclical psychodramas. It takes one to quit.

The need to blame rises from the fear of being blamed. Those who frequently blame others are avoiding the pain of chronic inner conflict. Before raising the condemning finger, the Blamer feels blame within. To follow this urge to punish the self is intolerable, so the punishment is turned outward. This rage against all inconvenience, all failure, all imperfection, all that goes wrong in life flares instantly and urgently within, flashes in the eyes, and burns in the words. Why feel blamed when you can blame?

Blame is evasive. Rather than face the difficulty and work to resolve it, it seeks transfer of the total package to the other, to stir up shame, pain, and self-rejection. Such negative means produce negative feelings and lead to negative results. Growth comes from owning responsibility, not from accepting blame.

Blame is censure. Rather than pointing toward the future

and inviting change and growth, blame penalizes the past and punishes the person for the acts, whether real or fantasized. Change and healing come from responsibility thinking, not from figuring out who's at fault.

Blame is powerless. Because it is punitive, negative, and evasive, blaming tends merely to increase the inner frustrations and conflicts in both parties that contributed to the original breakdown in communication or relationship. This leads to cyclical criticisms of each other, whether expressed in words or acted out in silence or submission.

Blaming occurs almost instinctively when we fall into the victim mode, ever seeking to bring the bad guy to justice for perceived wrongs done to us. However, this reaction only worsens the problem and can be a death blow to interpersonal relationships. If expressed, it can quickly lead to anger and all–out combat. Throughout this mess, any ideas of reaching a solution are abandoned.

Because blaming is a particularly insidious form of lying, use the confrontation technique to catch a Blamer in the act. Bring together the Blamer and the blamed party to arrive at the facts. The Blamer should be led to apologize to the person blamed. Repeat these gatherings as often as necessary until the Blamer recognizes the consequences.

THE BUSYBODY

Busybodies in corporate life are looking for attention and affection. They've learned to use confidential information to gain entry to conversations and social relationships. The more harmful the information to coworkers or current projects, the hotter its value for the Busybody. In some offices, the route of the Busybody is fixed, and his or her gossiping comes with the regularity of the lunch wagon.

Because the Busybody seeks social acceptance so desperately, his or her actions can be curtailed by the power of healthy relationships. A Busybody stops gossiping when he or she learns that important relationships—like the employer–employee relationship—depend on mutual trust.

Make the Busybody aware of the damage done to personalities, culture, and teamwork when information is leaked prematurely or in a distorted manner. Remind the Busybody of the trust placed in him or her by management, and how important that trust is to ongoing business relationships.

Sometimes we find a Busybody acting with anger and vengeance. This "Backstabber Busybody" builds temporary associations with other employees only to play them like pawns for personal advantage and advancement. Managers must act decisively to neutralize the Backstabber, who single-handedly can kill team spirit and mutual trust.

The activities of the Backstabber can't be rewarded in any way. On the contrary, a manager must play detective to find out who in the office is holding the bloody knife. This can be done most effectively by getting to know each employee well, perhaps by means of frequent get-togethers or breakfast meetings. When managers have established trust links to employees, any derogatory information received from a Backstabber can be checked out quickly and confidentially by going directly to the employee concerned.[2]

LARRY LAID-BACK

Those called Larry (or Lucy) Laid-Back are not so much sources of conflict as sources of frustration for managers. Conflict does often trail behind these people, however, because of their failure to really step up and accept responsibilities.

They cover themselves in most organizations by doing the absolute minimum. Larry Laid-Back is the bane of a company striving for excellence in a competitive world. Ironically, he thinks of himself as one of the better employees. He blames his inactivity on management, which he views as crazy, mixed-up, and unable to communicate what it really wants. His favorite expressions are:

> "It's not my job."
> "No one told me to do it."
> "I'm waiting for instructions."
> "I'm not being paid to do that."
> "It's not in my job description."
> "They haven't told me what to do."
> "It all pays the same."
> "The work will be there tomorrow."

This person thrives in a paternalistic state where the government steps in repeatedly to relieve people of individual responsibility. They multiply in bureaucracies where there is no individual accountability.

After all, as Peter Block points out:

> It is comforting to be led. It feels safe and implies a promise that if we follow, our future will be assured. The choice for dependency is a step into the mainstream along a conventional path. As organizations get larger, the need for coordination, control and consistency increases, and the unintended consequence is the proliferation of a dependent mind-set. The price we pay for dependency is our own sense of helplessness. Helplessness and waiting for clear instructions before acting are the death of the entrepreneurial spirit.
>
> Each of us has to decide—whose organization is this? If I want to feel a sense of ownership in this organization where I spend the best days of my life, I must confront my own wish for dependency and move in the direction of autonomy, knowing all along the way that I do have a choice and that, in fact, dependency may be the safer path.
>
> When we choose autonomy we realize that there is nothing to wait for. We do not require anything from those above us to create a unit or department of our own choosing. An autonomous or entrepreneurial mind-set means that I must commit myself to managing my team in a way that makes sense to me, and the weight of the organization is on my shoulders. It is heavy but it is also liberating.[3]

Having supervised people for over three decades, I believe most people are conscientious, hardworking, and willing to go the extra mile. It's been a privilege to associate with them. They've given their best and inspired me to give my best. I will always be grateful for them.

During this time, however, I've also seen a growing number of persons enter the workforce (or avoid it) with a totally passive attitude toward their own success or failure. Larry Laid-Back's favorite word is "They." "They" are supposed to take care of him, solve his problems, overlook his failures, keep him up with the cost of living, and make him a success.

Working with such persons is like pushing a rope uphill. The moment you stop pushing, there's no further progress.

I've come to believe that such individuals are the natural product of a society that has tried to create an environment of no consequences. In such an environment the following realities prevail:

- If I work, I receive money.
- If I don't work, I receive money.
- If I complete my work in the time allotted, I receive money.
- If I work overtime, I receive more money.
- If I do my homework, I'll get a passing grade.
- If I don't do my homework, I'll receive a passing grade anyway.
- If I do high-quality work, I'll succeed.
- If I do sloppy work, they'll correct it in Quality Control.
- If I don't commit a crime, I won't go to prison.
- If I commit a crime, I still won't go to prison for a first offense.
- If I give birth to a child out of wedlock, I'll receive money.
- If I give birth to a second child out of wedlock, I'll receive more money.

We must face the sobering possibility that we have begun to produce whole generations of these dependent people. Some of my colleagues are still comforting themselves with the delusion that "Young people are pretty much the same as they've always been" or "They were just as bad in my day."

Such persons need to read a sobering new study entitled *Beyond the Classroom: Why School Reform Has Failed and What Parents Need To Do*. This excellent study was conducted by Temple University professor Laurence Steinberg, University of Wisconsin psychologist Bradford Brown, and Stanford University sociologist Sanford Dornbusch. The ten-year research involving 20,000 high school students concluded that teachers are fighting a losing battle because teenagers today are far more influenced by apathetic parents and negative peer pressure.

Here are some of their findings:

- More than one third of the students said they get through the day by goofing off with friends.

- The average student spends less than an hour a day on homework, while students in other industrialized countries average four hours.
- Less than one in five students said good grades are important.
- Only about one in five parents consistently attends high school programs, and two in five parents have *never* been to one program.[4]

The authors conclude: "Our high school graduates are among the least intellectually competent in the industrialized world. . . . Systematic scientific evidence indicates quite compellingly that the problem of poor student achievement is genuine, substantial and pervasive across all ethnic, socioeconomic and age groups. . . . It is a problem of attitude and effort, not ability."[5]

In plain language, we are becoming one of the dumbest societies on earth. Still think nothing has changed? We have forgotten the first principle of behavioral psychology—you will always get more of whatever you reward. Or more importantly, the admonition of Scripture: "Do not be deceived, God is not mocked; for whatever a man sows, this he will also reap."[6]

THE GUERRILLA

The Guerrilla avoids face-to-face confrontation, preferring to take potshots at enemies through rumor and innuendo. To stay in the thick of things, he will often try to plant seeds of discord with comments such as "You really shouldn't let the boss take advantage of your good nature." Although the Guerrilla is the one with the problem, he or she will usually imply that others in the company share the view. Because he needs to tear others down to camouflage his own inadequacies, anyone's a potential target.

What sets Guerrillas apart from other difficult types is their hit-and-run tactics. They never confront the person with whom they have a problem (usually the leader). Instead they make oblique, hard-to-trace comments and then run for cover. Typical Guerrilla statements include:

"I'm very concerned about the boss. I wonder if everything's OK at home."

"Have you noticed anything going on between Mr. Smith and his secretary?"

"We need to pray for our minister. I think he's really struggling with a moral issue."

"I wish I could tell you the whole story, but I just can't."

This type of person is tough to deal with because he never really makes a specific charge. As a business executive, I always had a rule that if one staff member came into my office to complain about another, I would respond: "When you discussed this problem with him, what did he say?"

Of course, 99 percent of the time the problem had never been discussed with the other person. I would insist that this was the first responsibility.

The Guerrilla never engages in prolonged combat. This person is a verbal mugger. He or she drops devastating comments and moves on quickly. All of us can fall into the trap of verbal mugging.

We mug people when we're tired. Probably more than any other factor, fatigue can cause a conscientious individual to forget his values. Fatigue clouds our reason and lowers our guard. But mugging someone just because we're fatigued can leave lifelong scars.

We mug people because we're exasperated with them. They may have pushed our patience to an all-time limit. (What two-year-old doesn't do that daily?) We don't care about the consequences to their spirits, because we subtly feel that they deserve it.

We mug people because we're scared. Like cornered animals, we get desperate. In that condition, we often don't calculate what the results of our actions will be. We just want action, and we want it *now.*

Guerrillas can be deadly. They tend to create conflict and simultaneously drive it underground. All great organizations have a strong commitment that conflict must not go underground. It must be surfaced, ventilated, and resolved.

THE PREDATOR

I list the sexual Predator with the stealthy types not because he or she (usually he) is not fairly obvious but because too many organizations still do not take this offensive behavior seriously. It is often ignored or covered up, sometimes even by the victims.

Too often managers regard the victim as someone who needs to lighten up.

Organizations need clear policies stating that unwanted sexual advances or remarks that cause people to feel demeaned or uncomfortable are not allowed and will not be tolerated. The policy should then go on to spell out exactly what to do if harassed.

The Predator is someone who does not know when to stop pushing. He can't believe the other person really means no. Therefore, do not be coy or indirect. Give a straightforward response that cannot be misinterpreted.

When the Predator is the supervisor, the employee finds herself in a totally unfair position. Even if not stated, the implication is that compliance may be expected if she wants to hang on to her job.

Underlying the Predator lifestyle is a fundamental failure to treat all male and female colleagues with respect and dignity. To reduce a coworker to a sex object is immoral and illegal—and expensive! According to one survey, ignoring sexual harassment costs a typical Fortune 500 company as much as $6.7 million a year.[7]

Also at the root of the Predator lifestyle is emotional immaturity. Some men make a habit of expressing themselves sexually because they cannot express themselves emotionally. Ironically, the Predator is actually afraid of true intimacy.

Many organizations need to clean up their act with respect to terminology. Never refer to "the girls" in the office. We don't refer to "the boys" on the executive committee. Many women also dislike the term "ladies," since it conjures up images of drawing rooms and females playing a decorative role.

It's not really complicated. The opposite of "men" is "women." The opposite of "male" is "female." Be consistent and professional in your terminology. This has nothing to do with feminism. It's a simple matter of courtesy and respect.

THE PERFECTIONIST

This difficult person may not seem at first glance to be that much of a problem. He or she is neat, well-organized, immaculate in personal appearance. If you walk into his or her office, it will be carefully arranged and color coordinated. The pictures will be hanging straight, and any papers will be stacked neatly. If there are two stacks, they'll be at the same angle. Pull out the desk drawer—in one compartment will be large rubber bands, the second will have small rubber bands, and the third will have broken rubber bands to be repaired later.

I have a friend who is married to a Perfectionist. He swears that by the time he gets back from the bathroom in the middle of the night, she's got the bed made.

Their files are neat, color coded, and up-to-date. They are fanatical housekeepers and always put work ahead of play. They are frequently workaholics. They follow all rules and procedures. They live their entire lives nourished by a dream, that sometime there will be a whole day that goes perfectly. It never comes, but they keep hoping.

So why are such persons difficult? Why do they cause conflict —sometimes, serious conflict? There are a number of reasons.

A perfectionistic boss is impossible to please. No matter what you do, you only receive feedback on what you didn't do. It's a no-win situation.

Perfectionists are sometimes insensitive to others. Facts are more important than feelings. We've all suffered through a conversation in which one spouse attempts to tell an interesting story while the other constantly interrupts to make minor corrections. A Perfectionist cannot stand to overlook any fact he perceives to be erroneous, no matter how minor. He has no perspective. He can't tell the difference between a pimple and a tumor.

Perfectionists, surprisingly, waste large amounts of time. They spend thousands of hours getting things neat and organized so they can start on the really important things. That time never comes. There are always more minor things to get in order. They are more concerned about doing things right than doing the right things.

They are reluctant decision makers. They always want more data, more research. The process is more important than the product. Rather than make an imperfect decision, they make no decision. They order up yet another study. They inhibit progress rather than facilitate it. Talented staff become bored and restless because there's no movement. Believe it or not, this neat, well-groomed, well-organized person can keep an organization in an uproar.

how much they genuinely care about your desires and ultimate goals?

Dishonesty, for one thing.

"Acting in a way . . ." is precisely the point. No matter how often a person disagrees with your point of view on a particular issue or project, he won't express it. Nor will he volunteer any suggestions, points, or opinions he may have, if he thinks his ideas might possibly, perhaps, maybe conflict with yours.

The net result of this behavior is the loss of one more voice, one more independent source of potential benefit to the mix of ideas. All you're getting from these people are your very own ideas played back to you. If that's all you or your organization really needs, you can buy an audio cassette player for a lot less money, and a much smaller benefit package.

The leader who is surrounded by Yes Men and Yes Women is all alone. She or he might as well not have a staff. Any idea will be quickly ratified and celebrated. Such leaders drift into increasingly weird behavior. Strangely, they are not aware of it. The immediate feedback they receive from those around them is positive, enthusiastic—and terribly wrong.

I once heard former President Nixon speak to the International Affairs Club of New York City. A questioner asked him to give a thumbnail sketch of the state of the world. Nixon began with the Pacific Rim and worked his way around the world. Without notes he analyzed the internal political, social, and economic condition of virtually every major country on earth. I was spellbound. It was an incredible performance. I was watching a truly superior mind at work.

I couldn't help but wonder how a person of such obvious genius could have made such a colossal mess of his leadership role. I've come to believe that Nixon was done in, at least in part, by the Perpetual Pleasers. He staffed his White House with young people who were bright enough to do the job but not mature enough to incur the boss's wrath. No one would risk losing a high position by contradicting the fearsome leader. Instead of giving honest feedback, they groveled and prostituted themselves. No one would tell the emperor he had no clothes until it was too late.

George Schultz in a television interview was asked about the main requirements of being secretary of state. I'll always remember his wisdom: "The only person who can do a really important job is someone who doesn't have to have it. If you're desperate to keep the job, you can't do it."

I've learned the same thing in thirty years of consulting with senior executives in the business world. Those who were obsessed with keeping their jobs could never do the job. Those who were confident in themselves, comfortable with their weaknesses and strong in their convictions, were always the better leaders. They could express their disagreement clearly without attacking personally. Sometimes I saw it cost them their jobs. At least, it didn't cost them their souls. Usually, they went on to better jobs in healthier environments.

As a leader, be sure you always have some people around you who feel free to disagree with you no matter what. They will serve you well. They'll keep you from going over the cliff.

Even good marriages need disagreement. My wife says that whenever two people agree on everything, one of them is not necessary. Thus far in our three decades of marriage, we've both been highly necessary!

NOTES

1. Paul Meier, *Don't Let Jerks Get the Best of You: Advice for Dealing with Difficult People* (Nashville: Nelson, 1993), 168.
2. For a fuller description of liars, blamers, and backstabbers, see Leonard Felder, *Does Someone at Work Treat You Badly?* (New York: Berkley, 1993).
3. Peter Block, *The Empowered Manager* (San Francisco: Jossey-Bass, 1990), 186.
4. Laurence Steinberg, with Bradford Brown and Sanford M. Dornbusch, *Beyond the Classroom* (New York: Simon & Schuster, 1996), 18–20.
5. Ibid., 183–84.
6. Galatians 6:7, New American Standard Bible.
7. Leonard Felder, *Does Someone at Work Treat You Badly?* (New York: Berkley, 1993), 186.
8. David A. Seamands, *Freedom from the Performance Trap* (Wheaton, Ill.: Victor, 1991), 102–103.
9. Les Parrott, *High-Maintenance Relationships* (Wheaton, Ill.: Tyndale, 1996), 6.
10. Les Parrott as quoted in *Kansas City Star*, 1 September 1996.

PART TWO
WIN/WIN STRATEGIES

CHAPTER THREE

THE VALUE
OF GOOD
RECONNAISSANCE

In part one we met a menagerie: people in the office place
who can cause grief to us as managers. Where do these difficult people hang out in organizations? Where should we
look for them?

First, look in the mirror. Workers aren't the only difficult
people in the workplace; oftentimes managers instigate or contribute to conflict. Albert J. Bernstein and Sydney Craft Rosen
wrote a wonderful, entertaining book called *Dinosaur Brains*. In it
they describe the problems that can arise when managers operate from the primitive, instinctive, emotional part of the brain
that emphasizes self-preservation instead of genuine leadership.[1]

Difficult leaders are impulsive. They come up with big ideas
but don't follow through on the detail work. They are impatient
and cannot tolerate boredom. Sometimes they'll even invent
crises to satisfy their need for excitement. These "adrenaline
junkies" may become disappointed when their subordinates,
who have their own work and families to attend to, fail to rally
for the latest dilemma.

Difficult leaders live by the motto "Only the strong survive."
They think being tough, competitive, and aggressive is the only
way to get ahead, and making it to the top is their number one

goal. As a result, every conflict, no matter how small, is a power struggle. And the manager can't ever afford to lose.

Although they don't mind relegating grunt work to their underlings, difficult managers find it impossible to delegate authority. They want to hoard all the important tasks—and the credit—so they're seen as indispensable. As a result of their territoriality, they can become overwhelmed and waste a lot of time making expensive mistakes.

MENTORS OR TORMENTORS

My business partner and friend John Schuster says leaders come in one of two types: mentors and tormentors.

> Mentors are those who develop others; tormentors are those who diminish others.
>
> We all have had legitimate leaders in our lives, a teacher or relative or coach or boss who has left a permanent mark on our lives by giving us a frame of reference that we use continually. Such leaders are fondly recalled for the talent that they had in their followers. These are the leaders we emulate and want to model.
>
> Most of us have also had those in our lives who created self-doubt, fear and lack of confidence. These are the tormentors who make us take a solemn leadership vow: "If I ever get into a position like that I will remember never, ever to do that to anybody."
>
> Formative leaders, both good and bad, are the ones who help and hinder us on our own journey to leadership. The journey for each of us has been marked with victories and some defeats, glory and day-to-day plodding, team play and individual effort. What is well-known about accomplished adult learners and leaders is that the stories and episodes that we create and survive have to be reflected upon and woven into a life story that makes sense and has purpose. Leaders need to think over their stories for the lessons learned and find their unique gifts and assets. Once known and acknowledged, the gifts need to be packaged and committed to a purpose larger than the leader's ego, so that the ability to serve is cultivated.
>
> The lessons need to be passed on to others so that they can be guided into a discovery of their own talents and dreams, and be given the hope and courage to go out and create their own leadership journey.[2]

Not surprisingly, many difficult leaders are workaholics.

They don't value efficiency; all they care about is the number of hours an employee spends in the office. People who don't put in as many hours as they do are perceived as lazy, no matter how much work they actually accomplish. Workaholics are often perfectionists who are extremely irritable, and their irritability can make their employees resistant to everything they say.

OTHER PLACES TO LOOK

After you've taken a long, soul-searching look in the mirror, you're ready to start your tour of the following hangouts for difficult people:

If you're new to an organization, some of your strongest initial supporters, your first friends, and your earliest confidants may turn out to be the the most difficult to deal with.

In an educational or church setting, these will often be members of the search committee that selected you for the job. These people will likely feel a greater ownership of you because of the personal stake they have in your doing the job for which they hired you. They want to know that they made the right decision by bringing you on board. Getting close to you as fast as possible is the way they can affirm or discount their efforts.

In a corporate setting these persons may be your early mentors and coaches. They may resent your having advanced beyond their control. Your closest friend and confidant may turn into a Stamp Collector or a Busybody.

Granted, there is no need to be instantly suspicious of everyone who wants to befriend you. Being paranoid is no good for anyone. But do try to be aware of those people who seem to be working extra hard to gain your trust, secure your ear, and garner your attention.

Beware of the proverbial Trojans bearing gifts and giving special favors, as well as those people offering exclusive and allegedly sage advice. The advice may be mostly self-serving, and the adviser may quickly turn to critic if he feels his advice has not been heeded. Beware of expensive gifts; they come with strings attached.

The most difficult people you will have to deal with in the early going are often those who repeatedly compare you to the person who previously held your position of leadership. But that's not always detrimental. Even if they have nothing but praise for their former boss, that doesn't necessarily mean you'll suffer by comparison. In fact, as Marshall Shelley points out regarding pastors in a new church: "If they brag about their former pastor, it may be cause for thanks, not irritation. It's safer than the members skinning him alive. Members' attitudes about their former pastors can, in time, transfer to you."[3]

Unfortunately some people are always one leader behind in their loyalties.

One of the most likely breeding grounds for difficult people is an organization, department, or group where the official lines of authority do not match up with the path that decision making actually takes. Difficult individuals seem to arise in direct proportion to how divergent those two paths are. Shelley offers a prime example:

> One Minneapolis pastor who teaches a seminary course in practical theology asked his students to draw a chart of the lines of authority in their home churches. The students all drew neat boxes for various committees and boards with the lines running cleanly from one to another. Then he asked them to diagram the real decision-making process. One student turned in a sheet with lots of small circles around the edge connected to one large egg-shaped circle filling the center of the page. The large circle was labeled "Ralph."[4]

The "Ralphs" of the world love to move into a vacuum.

Another setting that frequently produces a difficult person is counseling. Leaders who try to help their employees solve personal problems run a real risk here, because people often seem to resent those who become too familiar with their intimate struggles. If the problems are not completely resolved, counselees dislike facing the counselor later—he not only knows their problem but is also aware it hasn't been solved.

When this happens in a company, the employee often resigns. When this happens with a pastor, the person often withdraws from the church physically or emotionally, or even works to oust the pastor.

This is why I strongly urge leaders not to be drawn into an extensive counseling relationship with their subordinates. The first thing you know, the employee has shared more personal information than he intended. Now he resents the leader for knowing more about his private demons than he meant for him or her to know. Not infrequently the counselee turns on the leader and tries to get rid of him.

As a corporate executive, I've sometimes had staff members begin to share facts about their personal lives that are outside the pale of a professional relationship. My normal practice has been to call time-out and say something like "I don't mean to be rude or uncaring, but I think this conversation is headed into an inappropriate area. I'm glad you have enough trust in me to share this type of problem, but I'm going to refer you to a professional counselor who will help you work through the difficulty. This way you'll get the help you need, and we can maintain a professional working relationship."

A corporation is not a clinic. As a manager you have a finite amount of time to accomplish a wide range of tasks. Your job is to refer, facilitate, and encourage the emotionally dysfunctional person to get help.

In my educational work with ministers, I even urge them to avoid more than two or three one-on-one counseling sessions with troubled parishioners. After that, clergy should refer the individual to a full-time counselor whose credentials and spiritual values they respect.

TIPS ON LEADING DIFFICULT PEOPLE

Wherever you come across the random Control Fanatic, the Martyr, the Blamer, or any other member of the menagerie, here are some mottoes to remember:

- When attacked by one, do not become one.
- Don't become preoccupied with a few difficult people.
- Learn from them; appreciate how and why they are different.
- Remember that failure is not fatal.
- Focus on building up the whole organization.
- Emphasize, encourage, and empower others.
- Continually reinforce productive leaders and members.
- Know the organization's unique history and values.
- Don't oversell your organization (in recruiting members, staff or volunteers).

- Build a healthy leadership team and stay close to the team-mates.
- Pray *for* the difficult people, not about them.
- Practice forgiveness. Forgiveness is an act of will, a conscious decision, not necessarily a feeling. It doesn't mean giving in and agreeing with the difficult person. It means letting go of the old wounds and making a new beginning.[5]

No matter how skilled a leader you are or what style you use, at times you will face conflict in the workplace. Research psychologists Kenneth W. Thomas and Ralph H. Kilmann have come up with five basic styles of conflict management: *avoiding, accommodating, competing, collaborating* and *compromising.* Like the different leadership styles, each conflict management style has its uses, and some work better in a given situation than others.

Thomas and Kilmann say that dealing with conflict always involves two dimensions: cooperativeness and assertiveness. The interaction of these two dimensions determines the style.[6]

Avoiding. As its name implies, when this style is used, the problem is simply avoided. It is best used with trivial problems or when a confrontation would do more harm than good. Avoiding is unassertive and uncooperative.

Accommodating. This style means you put the other person's concerns above your own. It is best used when you know you are wrong or that the problem is more important to the other person than it is to you.

Competing. If you need to make a quick or unpopular decision, this is a possible approach. Competing is the opposite of accommodating—it means you put your concerns above the other person's and do whatever is necessary to win. Competing is assertive and uncooperative. It should be used in a crisis or when the leader must make a strong decision based on principle.

Collaborating. The opposite of avoiding, collaborating involves working with the other person to find a solution that will fully satisfy both of you. When you collaborate, you admit that both parties' concerns are equally important, and you look for innovative ways to integrate both your perspectives. This style is both assertive and cooperative.

Compromising. Collaborating involves reaching a mutually satisfying solution. Compromising often results in a mutually unsatisfying solution, because both sides have to make concessions. Compromise splits the pie, while collaborating attempts to make the pie larger.

As authors Albert Bernstein and Sydney Rosen make clear, all managers have to learn to see employees as the company's most important investment. To better motivate employees and create a sense of loyalty, the authors offer the following suggestions:

- Don't issue orders; instead, sell the employees on a course of action. They'll feel more autonomous and respected.
- See yourself through their eyes. Would you want to work for you?
- Listen to them and remember what they say. Write it down if necessary.
- Set clear, reachable goals.
- Be consistent and follow through on your promises. Again, write them down if you need to.
- Make monitoring all employees a regular procedure. This way you can ensure the work is being done and stay on top of any problems that arise without specific employees feeling singled out and mistrusted.
- Never ridicule or publicly criticize employees.
- Delegate authority, not just grunt work.
- Offer new challenges and create opportunities for promotions.
- Show commitment and respect.
- Encourage co-workers to develop friendships.
- Use praise as a reward for a job well done.[7]

NOTES

1. Albert J. Bernstein and Sydney Craft Rozen, *Dinosaur Brains: Dealing With All Those Impossible People at Work* (New York: Wiley, 1989), 3–14, 18–21.
2. As quoted in Schuster Kane & Stevenin brochure, *Mastering Leadership*, 1997, n.p.
3. Marshall Shelley, *Well-Intentioned Dragons* (Carol Stream, Ill.: Christianity Today, 1985), 44.
4. Ibid., 45.
5. Ibid., 83–92.
6. Kenneth W. Thomas and Ralph H. Kilmann, *Thomas-Kilmann Conflict Mode Instrument*, booklet (Tuxedo, N.Y.: XICOM, 1991).
7. Adapted from Bernstein and Rozen, *Dinosaur Brains*, 136–40.

CHAPTER FOUR

GET YOUR SIGNALS STRAIGHT

T he scene is the northern coast of France in June of 1815, not far from the famous battle of Waterloo between Wellington and Napoleon. Two messengers, one for the British crown and one in the employ of Lord Rothschild, stand in the fog on the English side of the channel. They eagerly await the outcome of the battle.

Through their looking glasses a figure suddenly appears waving semaphore flags. Slowly the man spells out the words "Wellington defeated . . ." Immediately, the king's messenger leaps onto his horse and gallops toward London with the bad news.

Lord Rothschild's servant is a little more deliberate. Fog has now obscured his vision across the channel, and he decides to wait for confirmation.

In time the weather clears. The flags start up again, enabling him to receive the entire message: "Wellington defeated Napoleon."

THE MOST NEEDED SKILL

Clear, concise information is probably the most vital of all aspects of human interaction. When we try to communicate with problem people, we frequently stumble into misunderstanding. Basic to this is the tragically underemphasized art of listening.

Have you ever observed two people in a casual conversation—say, two Eternal Extroverts talking about their cars? One man carries on while the other holds his tongue for a slight pause in the dialogue when he can interject his own thoughts about his own car. It's almost as if the point of the entire conversation is not to learn but to get your next chance to speak. It really isn't a conversation at all. It's a frequently interrupted monologue. The conversants might as well be in different rooms. They do share one attribute, however: Neither is really listening.

Researchers tells us that we spend our time in communication as follows:

Writing	9%
Reading	16%
Talking	30%
Listening	45%

Yet, most of us have received little training in speaking clearly—and virtually none in listening. Our educational system spends most of its time training us to read and write. Thus, adult managers find their training in exactly reverse proportion to what is needed most.

Listening is so very vital to human interaction that, almost inevitably, when people are asked to list the attributes they find most satisfying in others, they put good listening near the very top. How many parents have heard their teenager cry, "You never listen to me!" Most parents say the same things about their offspring: Comments go "in one ear and out the other" or "They never hear a word I say." Perhaps both viewpoints have a ring of truth.

Being a good listener takes empathy, that is, the ability to relate to persons on their own level and try to see things from their point of view. Coauthors Kenneth Gangel and Samuel Canine define two attributes that help us achieve empathy and overall good communication: *mutuality*, consisting of responsibility shared by both parties to help a discussion succeed; and *self-disclosure*, an honest and candid revelation of the truth regarding oneself, including needs, desires, and goals.

They point out that both of these attributes require trust, the solid foundation upon which all good communication rests. Mutuality and self-disclosure not only enhance communication but also serve to alleviate what Gangel and Canine refer to as institutional tension. This tension is created when communication escalates beyond the participants' control. While these intensity levels (detectable by tone, word choices, and the number of interruptions) can be adjusted, a certain degree of tension may in fact always be present between a manager and those being supervised. But this should remain altogether manageable.[1]

FOUR WAYS TO LISTEN BETTER

When you interact with your staff, here are some elements of your job as a listener:

Focus. Try to keep your mind from wandering off the subject and away from the speaker. The most difficult aspect of this can be keeping your mind off yourself. Make little silent, internal comments to yourself, such as, *What is this person really talking about?*

Positive reinforcement or encouragement. This includes a lot of body language to convey that your attitude is warm and receptive to the subject at hand. Keep good eye contact, respond with short (usually monosyllabic) expressions that keep the speaker talking, and retain an attentive posture and smile. Most important, don't wear a poker face, for this implies a total lack of responsiveness.

Encourage the speaker to say more and continue speaking. This is a way to acknowledge your interest in the subject and your acceptance of how the speaker is presenting it. Good examples of encouraging statements are "Please, go on" or "Go ahead, tell me more."

Ask meaningful questions. A listener can help a speaker formulate and express ideas and feelings through active questioning, since even the most capable speaker often has difficulty bringing out what's on the inside. Open-ended questions, those not answerable with a simple yes or no, work best for this. The better worded the question, the better the answer will be.

Reflecting or paraphrasing. Restate parts of the discussion so the speaker can be assured that you understood what was spoken. Give it back in fewer words or more simple terms. You might begin with an expression like, "In other words, if I'm hearing you, you are saying that . . ."

Other good and bad habits in listening to your staff are summarized in the chart "Listening Well, Listening Poorly."

LISTENING WELL, LISTENING POORLY

Good Listeners . . .

. . . hold off on their judgments. They tend to be more controlled, listening for people to express their own unique needs.

. . . listen completely from the start of a conversation, trying to glean every nuance of meaning available. It is important for them to truly understand what is being said to them. This *enthrones* people.

. . . listen for both facts and feelings. They constantly reinforce the person who is speaking.

. . . always concentrate on the main issues. They know that you don't have to reply to everything that is said, and they refrain from sidetracking the issue with generalizing, off-topic, or sarcastic remarks.

. . . make every effort to concentrate on what is being said.

. . . take the conversation one step at a time. They realize that active listening is a full-time job and give all their attention to it.

Poor Listeners . . .

. . . tune out the other person from the beginning, often jumping to a conclusion about what's coming before it's said.

. . . spend time preparing their next statement instead of truly paying attention.

. . . concentrate mainly on the facts, always looking for specific bits of information to be used as ammunition against the other person in order to win an argument.

. . . have to respond to everything. This creates the climate of a contest, with responses usually intended to gain a sort of superiority over the other person.

. . . will fake attention and interest. (This is often detected.)

. . . divide their attention, especially if they are busy or feel rushed.

BAD HABITS

The following mistakes have tripped us all at one time or another. A great deal of embarrassment and unnecessary conflict can be avoided if we lay these habits aside:

Criticizing. The clumsy or untimely use of criticism can do untold damage to an otherwise healthy relationship. Often taking the form of a rude interruption, criticism has a tendency to put a speaker on the defensive, which can change the entire course of a discussion.

Praising. While seemingly harmless, praise can fall prey to bad timing as easy as constructive criticism. It can divert a speaker's attention from the subject. Also, it may convey that the listener isn't really "tracking" with what the speaker was saying. It can even irritate, especially if interjected too early and before the speaker delivers what he or she believes to be the most important point.

Diverting. This is a keen irritation for any speaker. By deliberately altering the course of the conversation, important points can be missed entirely.

Reassurance. Although at times appropriate, reassurance can also have a "blowback" effect that is totally opposite of what the reassuring party may have intended. For instance, if a listener suddenly halts the speaker to say, "Don't be nervous now," the speaker may start asking internal questions such as, *Do I appear that nervous?* Now, instead of flowing along smoothly, the speaker is second-guessing himself. The listener has created the very nervousness he sought to avoid.

Advising. Advice not sought is about as welcome as an IRS knock on the front door. By interrupting a speaker with little gems of your knowledge, a listener can damage credibility and cause uncertainty.

Ordering. Managers are more often guilty of this one than others. In the course of a dialogue, the manager suddenly blurts out, "I thought we covered that already!" The speaker is naturally put on the defensive.

Labeling or stereotyping. This is a form of discounting. If I can classify you as left-wing or right-wing or moderate, I no longer have to listen to you.

Excessive questioning. This is mostly just annoying. Use questions only when necessary (write them down and wait until an appropriate time). Keep your questions clear and concise in a manner that will not raise tempers. Some people ask non-question questions, such as "Don't you really mean that . . . ?" This is not asking a question; it's injecting one's own opinion.

QUESTIONS THAT SUCCEED

If questions are something of a double-edged sword, especially coming from a boss, what kinds of things can we ask that will help communication rather than frustrating it? Here are three: open-ended questions, reflective questions, and directive questions.

1. *Open-ended questions.* General in nature, these are fashioned to elicit wide-ranging responses on broad topics. They usually begin with the traditional *what, why, who, how,* or *tell me about . . .*

Open-ended questions intentionally involve the personal and professional opinions of the person to whom they are directed. They fundamentally try to get another person to open up and tell you what he or she thinks on a certain topic. Here are some examples:

"Tell me about a challenge you faced in a previous job."

"How do you like to be managed?"

"Where do you want to find yourself in a year (three years, etc.)?"

"What kind of people rub you the wrong way in work situations?"

"How do you deal with the stress of deadlines?"

"What types of work bring you the most satisfaction?"

"Tell me what you liked and didn't like about your previous job."

"What matters most to you in your professional life?"

"Upon being hired, what can you offer this company immediately?"

"What skills or abilities can we help you develop?"

2. *Reflective questions.* You use reflective questions like a mirror when you want to clarify how a person thinks or feels. Reflective questions minimize the natural isolation of every human being. They require both careful and selective listening. Careful, because your own preconceptions of what the other person is trying to express can taint your interpretation of what is actually being said. Selective, because in order to get the gist of what is

being communicated you must sort out the main ideas and feelings from the incidental.

3. *Directive questions.* With directive questions you keep the two-way communication going by narrowing the problem to a manageable size and building consensus upon disputed territory. They can be dressed with positive activators such as "Since we agree on . . ." or "You've said you liked _____, so how about . . ." In this way the other person can be nudged into committing to a certain position, thus furthering the chances for a viable solution to the problem.

A MASTER PLAN

Where we are headed with all these techniques is the better understanding of one another, resulting in a more effective workplace. If you want a master plan to hold in your mind as the words fly around your head, remember these four letters: C–I–A–C.

Clarify
Interpret
Agreement
Consensus

These are the four main steps of working through a difficulty with any problem employee.

Clarify. Try to get the big picture of what you're dealing with. Ask questions (preferably open-ended) to gather all the input you can. Don't stop the minute you think you've got a grasp of the situation. If an employee begins with, "You don't understand . . ." try replying with, "It's quite possible that I don't understand. Please explain it to me in your own words."

Interpret. Now give the content back in your own words through reflective questions or statements. Cover every possible angle in your reiteration of the problem. "Tell me if I'm getting this right. . . ."

Agreement. A high priority should be to find some common ground. This will keep the conflict from escalating and move all those involved toward a solution. Remember to focus on empathy, not sympathy. Sympathy says, "I feel like you feel." Empathy says, "I comprehend how you feel."

Consensus. Now you can build on the common ground that

has been explored. Here you can more easily introduce possible solutions and deal with the actual elements of the problem. "OK, so we're in agreement that . . . How about if we try to . . . ?"

Consensus is not achieved through voting. Consensus is not achieved by imposing win–lose outcomes. Consensus is not dictating the conclusion. Consensus is not giving in.

Rather, consensus is sharing ideas.

Consensus is discussing, evaluating, and debating. Consensus is organizing and prioritizing information. Consensus is struggling to reach the best conclusion together.

Consensus is the entire group being open to the best solution as it emerges.

Properly applied, the C–I–A–C method is an excellent tool for maintaining good, open lines of communication during a conflict.

LET THE PLAN SUCCEED

As you move along, here are a few "don'ts" in communication.

- Don't be drawn into arguments. Ultimately no one wins a real argument.
- Don't try to be an expert on everything. Let those with a good grasp of the subject matter have their own say. Our unique experiences and perspectives as human beings make us excellent sources of information for each other if we can just learn to keep our mouths shut long enough for others to speak their piece. Besides, nothing is more irritating than a know–it–all.
- Don't overanswer an objection or question. You may be able to sway another person to accept your position through a logical argument. But the debate can quickly turn emotional if a manager tries to grind the opposition into the dust.
- Don't get sidetracked on irrelevant subjects—no matter who initiates the diversion. This only exacerbates the problem and may place a solution permanently out of your reach.
- Don't cast doubt on your own answer. A manager under-

mines his or her own authority by second-guessing. You don't have to say, "That may not be a very good answer" or "Maybe I'm wrong, but . . ."

• Don't feel you must answer every statement. Sometimes silence is not only golden, it is vital. Especially when dealing with emotional issues, there's merit in merely sitting and listening. Quite often an employee will intermingle personal feelings in a professional discussion, and you have to be able to distinguish the two.

Communication is a most vital tool to guiding and resolving conflicts and problems. As long as people work together they must communicate. Run down this list of communication behaviors and see which side you tend to favor:

Increase Success	Block Success
Listen	Disagree
Paraphrase	Be impatient
Accept	Argue
Credit and thank	Defend
Praise others	Get turned off
Recognize ideas	Nitpick
Stay open to suggestions	Don't listen
Stay willing	Complain
Be informed	Disapprove
Be aware	Question motives
Seek usefulness	Tell "war stories"
Trust	Be hurt
Esteem others	Sulk
Show approval	Take offense
Acknowledge adequacy	Become bored
Seek comprehension	Don't think
Be honest	Become tired
Build	Shoot down
Laugh	Take everything literally

NOTE

1. Kenneth O. Gangel and Samuel L. Canine, *Communication and Conflict Management in Churches and Christian Organizations* (Nashville: Broadman, 1992).

CHAPTER FIVE

WHEN LIFE GETS TOXIC

You may find it hard to believe (I doubt it), but there are times in business when the previous two chapters don't cover all the bases. Your best reconnaissance fails you, and your most sincere attempts to communicate fall short. You wind up face-to-face with a Dominant Dictator who wants to take over your operation, or a Chronic Liar who is looking you straight in the face with determination to maintain his falsehood.

Before you know it, you are just plain annoyed. And the employees you're trying to deal with are worse than that; they're steaming. Fumes are rising, and they're not coming from your plant's chemical research lab. They're coming out of people's ears and from the cracks between their clenched teeth.

Now what? Once anger gets going, is there any way to redeem a win/win resolution?

TECHNICAL GIANTS, EMOTIONAL DWARFS

Despite our feeling-oriented culture, many of us are poor at expressing feelings—good or bad. How many fathers cannot say "I love you" to their sons or daughters? How many marriages go years without the partners affirming and expressing their appreciation? Managers constantly tell me they get tied in knots trying to give an employee a simple compliment. In the business world I continually see technological giants and emotional dwarfs.

Spend an evening watching television (if you can stand it). You'll see horrible ways of dealing with anger. No wonder many of us have concluded that expressing any frustration must be avoided at all cost.

The first thing to understand about anger is that it's not optional. You cannot choose never to experience anger. It is a basic human emotion along with love, joy, fear, and sadness. Who would want to live in a world devoid of feelings?

Feelings are an indispensable part of our lives. Losing the ability to feel is tragic, certainly more grave than losing our sense of touch, taste, or smell. Only when we are in touch with our feelings are we able to control them.

I believe that inadequately processed anger is one of the most common problems in business today. Helping a person recognize and deal constructively with hurts and offenses is among the most important things I can do as a leader. If an employee is able to handle anger, he or she will probably mature in other aspects of life and be fairly free from emotional difficulty.

George Washington often reminded the nation that "Government, like fire, is a useful servant, and a dreadful master." The same can be said for conflict and anger.

Neither conflict nor anger are inherently evil. Jesus was in constant conflict with the social and religious structures of His day. He is described more than once as being angry. On the other hand, anger makes us more vulnerable to crossing the line into hurtful, destructive behavior. Uncontrolled anger is the deadly nerve gas of conflict.

One organization I consulted has adopted the rule of the four "P's":

> *Position:* It is okay to take a position different from others or the majority of the team. You will not be devalued for doing so.
>
> *Potency:* It is okay to express your views powerfully, with strong conviction.
>
> *Persuasion:* It is okay to try to persuade others of the logic or rightness of your position.
>
> *Personal Attack:* It is not okay to attack another leader personally, to demean his or her intelligence, or question the person's integrity.

This philosophy has stood them in good stead through years of change, growth, and conflict.

UNHEALTHY WAYS TO DEAL WITH ANGER

Be careful not to deal with anger by using one of the four D's: *denial, diversion, delay,* or *dilution.* Those four D's represent uhealthy responses to anger, as we shall see.

Denial. Have you ever had a red-faced, out-of-control person literally scream at you and say, "I am not angry!"

The paradox is that although anger obviously abounds in our society, it is not socially acceptable. Like conflict in general, anger is viewed as a bad thing. That is why denial is often the first response.

The personal benefits are obvious: If you deny the existence of your anger, then there is no need to deal with it! Perhaps you label it frustration or irritation or hurt or anxiety or one of the more acceptable emotions.

The more we fail to deal with our anger, the more powerful and destructive it becomes. Dr. Theodore Rubin in *The Angry Book* refers to it as the "slush fund."

> The more we push down anger, the more it accumulates. This accumulated anger will then express itself through . . . camouflages . . . or it may convert its energy to more recognizable forms. It can lead to such symptoms as guilt, obesity, or insomnia. It can manifest itself in psychosomatic illnesses like backache, dermatological conditions, headaches, gastrointestinal symptoms and ulcers. Other possible manifestations are sexual problems and fatigue.[1]

Diversion. This is redirecting your anger toward a more acceptable target. Since I don't want to tell off the board chairman, I attack my spouse or children.

Taking your anger out on any innocent bystander is counterproductive. Similarly, taking your anger out on inanimate objects, like doors, walls, and furniture, is diverting your anger from the source to the peripheral. Is it the wall you're angry with? Did the dog offend you?

Delay. Sometimes we try to postpone our anger, laughing it off or forcing it from our minds with exercise, alcohol, drugs, or workaholism. Other times we put off thinking about it until later —and then we really start to stew.

Dilution. Finally, we may try to tell ourselves we don't have the right to get mad; that the other person can't help his behavior; that rational people keep cool under all conditions.

Denial, diversion, delay, and dilution are unhealthy ways to deal with anger because they don't resolve anything. Anger is energy; it has to be converted or directed. It doesn't just evaporate. If you don't learn this, it could cost you your life.

According to David Glass:

> Hostility is listed as one of the three major components of coronary-prone behavior, which tends to greatly increase one's chances of a heart attack. Patients with chronic pain syndromes also show increased levels of anger. The various types of patients, illnesses and physical symptoms are probably legion.
>
> In addition to the physical symptoms created by bottled-up anger, there are the more obvious emotional symptoms like depressions, neuroses, psychoses, and potentials for murder and suicide. This is not to imply that unresolved hurts and anger are the sole cause of all these symptoms, but they certainly comprise a major cause.
>
> It is interesting to note that 60 percent of all homicides occur among family members—the home being the place where feelings are most apt to erupt. The most likely victim is usually one's spouse, lover, or friend.[2]

Our national immaturity in dealing with conflict and anger has made us one of the most violent societies on earth. The statistics reflect a sad reality of mishandled, misdirected behavior:

- Child abuse. Abuse affects 1.4 million American children each year. This figure covers physical abuse only, not neglect.
- Spouse abuse. One of every 22 American women will be a victim of physical violence during a given year.
- Homicide. There are 9.8 homicides for every 100,000 Americans, 2.7 homicides for every 100,000 Canadians.
- Rape. There are 41 *reported* rapes for every 100,000 Americans, 11.8 reported rapes for every 100,000 Canadians. The actual incidence is believed to be many times higher.

ANGER'S HIDDEN FRUIT: DEPRESSION

Depression is anger turned inward. It is a silent temper tantrum that often results in a loss of self-esteem, delusions, unreal expectations, and isolation. Depression has other outcomes too, including:

- drug abuse
- alcohol abuse
- a severely diminished ability to love
- gambling
- hurting others by hurting yourself
- impulsive spending
- selfishness
- reckless risk-taking

Repressing anger is like throwing yourself on a grenade. Sure, you save the platoon, but you become the victim when most likely you had a reason to be angry in the first place.

According to Piaget, 90 to 95 percent of all clinical depressions are anger-related.[3] Clearly, to avoid depression and other such maladies (ulcers, tension headaches), we must learn to deal with our anger in a more healthy way.

DEALING WITH ANGER

Understanding your own anger will not enable you to handle all the angers of the world, but you will know how to keep your own from working against you.

Step one: the situation. Recognize your anger. You're not "hurt," you're angry. Admit it. Then determine what it stems from. Ask whether your position is perhaps unreasonable. Does your opponent have a point?

Step two: the source. Identify the source of your anger. Examine your behaviors. Did you contribute to the problem? If so, avoid humiliating or belittling yourself. Instead, define the pain you're experiencing. Are you overreacting? Did you take it personally when it wasn't meant that way?

Step three: the solution. Be realistic. Give yourself some time. Don't try to solve a problem when you are furious.

Once you're in control of yourself, talk to the other person.

Do not talk about their attitude; talk about their behavior and how it made you feel. Propose a solution.

Finally, schedule a later time to talk about it. But don't let yourself or the other person off the hook. If there's no progress, consider bringing in a third party.

WHY IS THIS SO HARD?

If you consistently have trouble dealing with anger, you may need to retrace your past. Dr. Leonard Felder suggests ways that your own personal history can interfere with how you respond in the workplace.

> Imagine an angry co-worker screaming at you. If you grew up in a household where anger was not expressed, you might feel you don't have the tools or experience to deal with this person. If, on the other hand, you grew up with an explosive, hot-tempered parent whose anger terrified you, you might feel you need to avoid or be extra cautious with this angry screamer at your job.
>
> If you have an explosive temper of your own, you might feel provoked by this person, and yet you probably realize that your own temper could get you fired or cost you in other ways.[4]

If you have felt mistreated in the past and you try to make up for all past injustices by lashing out at this current enemy, you might find your response gets you nothing but trouble.

Psychologist and speaker Gary Oliver urges men, especially, to identify their specific anger pattern.[5] Recognize the symptoms, he notes. There may be tension (veins sticking out of neck), increased pulse, becoming red in the face, or talking faster, louder or lower. There may be sweaty palms, churning stomach, hiding, avoiding other people, or being confrontational.

The point is we need to be able to identify anger in ourselves. This is not as easy as it sounds. Although most of us know ourselves well enough to know and adjust for the warning signs of anger, many have no idea they're angry until they erupt like Mount St. Helens, spewing fire and ash over everything within a several-mile radius.

We need to be on the lookout for people and situations that make us respond with anger. Because when we have lost control, it will likely be far too late to do anything reasonable about it.

Let's be as clear as possible: Conflict is not evil in itself. Neither is anger. Intense anger injected into intense conflict, however, often leads to evil. Don't ever buy the shallow concept that you have a right to act any way you feel like—that, after all, you're just "expressing yourself." Nonsense. Self-control is still a virtue. In management, it's an absolute necessity.

I was in a plant the day after we had conducted a seminar on "Behavioral Management Through the Use of Consequences." A foreman burst into the room and said: "Dr. Stevenin, I got the point of that class. I just went out there and uncorked a consequence this one guy will never forget!"

I looked at this man, who was red-faced, sweating, veins throbbing on the side of his neck, and realized he had just blown up. He had loudly, personally attacked an employee on the shop floor within the hearing of others. He had, in fact, violated a major emphasis of the seminar—never try to give corrective feedback to others when you are emotionally out of control.

We sat down and talked about it. I explained to him what was probably going on out in the plant. As soon as he stormed off, the man's fellow workers surrounded him and asked: "What's wrong with the foreman?"

Notice carefully the wording of that question.

Not "What did you do wrong?"

Not "Did you make a big mistake?"

But "What's wrong with the foreman?"

As a leader, anytime you lose control, in the eyes of the troops you become the problem, no matter how outrageous the provocation.

The story often gets even worse. Surrounded by his peers, the attacked worker may begin to fabricate a conversation that never took place. (If you don't know that employees sometimes do this, you should.)

"I'll tell you what I told him. I told him he could take this job . . ."

"Wow, did you say that?"

"Yes, and furthermore I told him that . . ."

"Wow, you said that, too?!"

In reality, this conversation between worker and boss never occurred. But the employee is seizing the opportunity to regain lost stature. While the foreman is in the office congratulating himself for straightening out this worker, the employee is getting positive strokes from his peers for causing management to lose control.

I've been in some businesses where the atmosphere was so adversarial that the favorite indoor sport of workers was to try to get management to jump the emotional tracks. Each time it happened, some employees felt they had scored points.

Here is my strong advice to managers: Never, never, never try to give corrective feedback when you are out of control. You'll lose every time. No matter what the *original* problem, you'll *become* the problem.

Go for a walk. Postpone the discussion for an hour, or even a day. Get your act together. Prepare to identify the specific behavior (not the attitude) that was unacceptable.

Be prepared to hear the employee's version of events in case you misunderstood. Outline specific steps that must be taken to correct the problem. Let him know you will hold him accountable for improvement. When he leaves your office, he should be saying, "I have a problem," NOT "The boss has a problem."

Notice the emphasis on behavior. Did you ever visit with an employee about his or her "poor attitude"? In my experience, it's a waste of time. Most people think their attitude is perfectly understandable in view of all they have to put up with, including me, the leader! Furthermore, when I visit with them about it, it usually gets worse.

The problem is that attitude is undefinable. Instead of discussing attitude, I've learned to discuss specific unacceptable behaviors and then outline improved behaviors that must be implemented.

Once I called two staff members into my office and said something like "I know you don't like each other. It's okay not to like each other. You're not required to like each other. What you *are* required to do is to behave toward each other as if you liked each other during the working day. You must communicate. You must keep each other informed. You must stop running each other down."

I literally drew up a behavioral contract outlining what each one must do and must not do. I asked them to sign it and make a commitment to fulfill their obligations to each other. They both agreed.

Guess what I discovered a few weeks later. They were starting to like each other! (Of course, now they had serious reservations about me.)

That was OK, too. I was the leader in that situation. A leader must get his or her security from something besides popularity. Sometimes the leader must sacrifice total approval to rescue others from themselves.

Joseph Stowell, president of the famed Moody Bible Institute of Chicago, says in an excellent book entitled *Loving Those We'd Rather Hate* that it is helpful to ask yourself when you're most likely to be angry. Before your morning coffee? As soon as you get home from work? Before you settle in at the office? Don't let situations control your emotions. Examine your behaviors. Are you displacing your anger or transferring it to someone else (such as the cop who gave you the ticket)?

In addition, avoid humiliating or belittling yourself. Stowell writes: "The best time to deal with anger is before you get angry. Many people have found that if they wait until they are actually angry, it's too late to deal positively with the emotion."[6]

FACING THE DRAGON

When a visibly angry person confronts you, it's normally best to allow him or her to ventilate that anger. Angry people always have what I call "The Speech" ready to go. They've worked on it, polished it, rehearsed it. I guarantee you someone is going to get it—the sooner the better.

To help avoid an explosive confrontation, lead the person into a private office or area and, if possible, have him or her sit down. Then let him give the entire speech uninterrupted and unchallenged.

While he's speaking, maintain an active listening posture. Stand or sit still, and keep your body language open. Don't cross your arms across your chest. Maintain eye contact and nod occasionally, maintaining an expression of concern. Take notes and make appropriate, short, active–listening statements such as "Please tell me more" and "And then what happened?"

Active listening also involves rephrasing the person's concerns so he knows you understand his meaning. You might begin your rephrasing with "Let me see if I understand what you're saying . . ." or "It sounds as if you're concerned about . . ."

Once you're sure you understand why the person is angry,

pause briefly before you continue with questions. If it's appropriate, apologize or tell him you empathize with his concerns. Then make empathy statements such as "I'm glad you told me," "I see what you mean," "I'd feel the same way if that happened to me."

Never bottle up the speech or try to cut it short. In fact, encourage the whole speech. At the end you might ask, "Is there anything else bothering you that you haven't told me?"

While you're dealing with the angry person, recognize your own emotions but stay in control of them. The person may try to make you angry by using profanity, sarcasm, personal attacks, or name-calling. It is okay for you to become angry in response to another person's outrageous behavior, but it is not okay to lose control of your own behavior. As Rollo May said, "Freedom is the capacity to pause between the stimulus and the response, and in the process to choose."

Remember that the angrier a person is, the less reasonable he is. After you've given him a chance to fully vent and he has calmed down, propose possible solutions to the problem.

Steven Susser also recommends that the two parties talk behind closed doors and resist the urge to respond to anger with anger. Most often, anger only begets more anger.

But what about people who are so angry they are screaming at you? They may even cross the line from verbal abuse to physical abuse.

Here are some approaches I've used. None of them works perfectly, but they can help.

"Time out. I'd really like to help you, but I need to ask you to slow down and calm down."

"John, I'm sorry, but you are clearly out of control. We need to bring this conversation to an end for now until you're in shape to talk about this." *Note:* Stick to it. Don't let the person talk you into going on. His rage will only accelerate even higher.

"You're being so abusive that I'm concerned about my own safety. I'm going to bring our security officer into the room."

Don't think you will never have to do this. Workplace violence is becoming a major problem. You cannot help others unless you have a healthy respect for yourself and your own value as a human being.

PERSONAL TRIGGERS

We all have certain things that trigger our anger. In the interests of being transparent, I'll give you my personal list.

Discounting—devaluing my idea before I've even had a chance to explain it.

Stereotyping—assuming that because I'm male, or middle-aged, or white, or conservative, that I must have a certain view or attitude on a given issue before we've even discussed it.

Name-calling—which usually comes from a person who is out to inflict damage and is out of control. This doesn't make it easier to take.

Profanity—especially taking God's name in vain. Here's an oddity—people who would not even consider using the more vulgar words will habitually abuse God's name, although it is specifically forbidden in the Ten Commandments.

Sarcasm—this can draw me into anger at warp speed. It's the ultimate put-down couched in hurtful humor.

BUSINESS TRIGGERS

In my consulting practice, I train retailers and others who deal with the public to be aware of using "triggers" or "snarl words" that frequently produce anger with customers. Here are some of the worst:

"That's not in my department."
"You'll have to . . ."
"It's perfectly obvious to me . . ."
"Let me tell you . . ."
"How many times do I have to tell you . . . ?"
"That's just our policy."
"I totally disagree with you."

Such snarl words can be converted into smile words:
"Let me put you in touch with . . ."
"Would you be good enough to . . . ?"
"Here's an idea I'd like to get your opinion on."
"Let me make a suggestion . . ."
"Here's an alternative . . ."

A psychiatrist who has examined hundreds of prisoners

convicted of murder says 70 to 80 percent of them didn't want to hurt anyone, and they never seemed to get angry or to have any problem with anger. They were often law-abiding citizens who didn't even have a traffic ticket to their record. What happened?

In his opinion, they allowed small amounts of anger to build in their unresolved "slush fund." One slight provocation was then enough to make the fund overflow and cause them to explode, usually taking out their violent feelings on someone they knew.

EMOTIONS R US

I believe that one of life's most important abilities is to be aware of our own feelings. Many of us, particularly those with religious backgrounds, have been virtually robbed of the right to our feelings, especially feelings of anger. It's a sort of psychological rape, in which a vital part of our humanity is violated, leaving us with irreparable emotional damage.

We need to reprogram our anger messages:

From "Anger is bad"   to "Anger happens."
From "Anger is dangerous"   to "Anger can be controlled."
From "Anger is unacceptable" to "People get angry"
                                 (anger is universal).

Our emotions, particularly anger, need not dominate our lives. As psychology professor Archibald Hart writes:

> I repeat, we are not superhumans. We do not have to be dominated and disturbed by our emotions. We also need not be so afraid that we avoid them. Emotions must be woven into our . . . lives in such a way that they produce a harmonious and complementary pattern of wholeness. Our emotions are not in conflict with our spirituality. Emotions themselves are not sinful. They do not have to disturb our spiritual well-being but can be used to complement and enhance it.[7]

THREE RESPONSES TO CRITICISM

Response	Thought	I Feel	Behavior	Possible Outcome
"I'm no good."	"I'm always goofing up. I'm worthless."	Sad, anxious, hurt, depressed, fearful, threatened, lonely, disappointed, withdrawn, worthless	Isolation, moping, giving up, crying, silence, chemicals, stop eating	Lie in bed; avoid work; put myself down; sink into depression; seek chemical supports; violate my own values. Slam myself and repeatedly ask, "Why me?" Self-debasement. Consider inflicting physical damage on self. Think, "The world would be better off without me," or "I'm no good to anybody; nobody cares."
"He's no good."	"That stupid man is on my back again."	Angry, frustrated, want to get even, want to run away, unfairly treated, fearful, threatened	Obscenities, accusations, destruction, chemical crutch, fast driving, slacking off, getting "sick," breaking rules, quitting	I fume for days and don't think clearly or rationally. Tell myself the world is no good. I'm right and "they're" wrong. Destroy property. Hurt myself trying to get even.
Healthy	"Here's a chance to learn something."	Secure, comfortable, warm, satisfied, content	Review in what ways I may have been goofing up. Do I see who truly has the problem?	Define the problem(s) and identify solutions. Experience confidence and a feeling of elation. Others appear satisfied with the way I handled the situation. I'm satisfied, too.

CRITICISM AND ANGER

Another anger trigger for me can be criticism, especially:

• Criticism I know is wrong
• Criticism I know is right
• Continuous criticism from one source
• Criticism when I am tired, sick, or overwhelmed with personal problems

The chart "Three Responses to Criticism" (see page 85) shows three ways we can react to criticism. Study the chart to see how the only healthy response to criticism is to view the criticism as an opportunity to learn about a problem and to solve it.

Despite the destructiveness of uncontrolled, negative anger, some of us are actually reluctant to give it up. Frederick Buechner reminds us:

> Of the Seven Deadly Sins, anger is possibly the most fun. To lick your wounds, to smack your lips over grievances long past, to roll over your tongue the prospect of bitter confrontations still to come, to savor the last toothsome morsel of both the pain you are given and the pain you are giving back—in many ways it is a feast fit for a king. The chief drawback is that what you are wolfing down is yourself. The skeleton at the feast is you.[8]

How does one keep from this self-devouring? People of faith have a secret weapon in the struggle against toxic warfare—the almost lost art of forgiveness.

Forgiveness is not suddenly turning warm and fuzzy toward the offending individual. It is an act of the will. That is why the well-known Lord's Prayer includes the line "Forgive us our debts as we also have forgiven our debtors."

People may not deserve my forgiveness—but I deserve to be rid of the offense. I need to be rid of the complications involved in keeping that anger, that grudge, that hatred inside me.

POSITIVE ANGER

Up until now we've looked at anger as a problem to be dealt with, a potential bomb to be defused. But anger does have its positive applications.

Used sparingly, anger can motivate us to get ourselves out of a bad situation or prompt others to act. Bernstein and Rosen describe several instances in which expressing anger had positive results in the workplace. For instance, a man discovered that he had been cheated by a supplier for years. He became angry and stopped doing business with the company.

In another case, a project had become logjammed, and department heads kept holding useless meetings in which nothing new was accomplished. By verbalizing his anger with the whole mess, one employee was able to get the project moving.[9]

It's important to note that anger gets results only when it's an unusual response. If you're constantly getting mad and blowing up, people will soon see you as a blowhard and stop paying attention.

To determine whether your anger is a positive force, Bernstein and Rosen suggest you consider the following factors:

- Frequency—normal people lose their temper less than once a month.
- Focus—know what it is specifically that you're mad at.
- Proportion—don't make mountains out of molehills.
- Direction—confront the people you're angry with; don't take out your anger on others.
- Repetition—don't keep getting worked up over the same old problems.
- Duration—don't hold grudges.
- Style—never use name-calling; say what *you feel.*
- Audience—confront people in private; avoid public displays of anger.
- Time orientation—deal with the present, not the past.
- Reciprocity—when you get angry, accept that others may get angry back.
- Evidence—don't read people's minds; make sure you are angry at them for a real offense.
- Controllability—be careful not to lose it.[10]

Mature managers are fully aware of the environment around them and their own feelings, including feelings of hurt and anger.

They accurately determine the reasons for the feelings. They have no unresolved anger in their "slush fund."

The mature person responds by choice rather than by reaction.

NOTES

1. Theodore Isaac Rubin, *The Angry Book* (London: Macmillan, 1969), 24.
2. David Glass, *Behavior Patterns, Stress and Coronary Disease* (Hillsdale, N.J.: L. Erlbaum Assoc., 1977), n.p.
3. Gerald W. Piaget, *Control Freaks* (New York: Dell, 1991), 186.
4. Leonard Felder, *Does Someone At Work Treat You Badly?* (New York: Berkley, 1993), 72–73.
5. Gary J. Oliver, *Real Men Have Feelings Too* (Chicago: Moody, 1993), 134–36.
6. Joseph Stowell, *Loving Those We'd Rather Hate* (Chicago: Moody, 1994), 131–32.
7. Archibald D. Hart, *Unlocking the Mystery of Your Emotions* (Dallas: Word, 1989), 2.
8. Frederick Buechner, *Wishful Thinking* (San Francisco: HarperCollins, 1993), 2.
9. Albert J. Bernstein and Sydney Craft Rosen, *Dinosaur Brains* (New York: Wiley, 1989), 119–24.
10. Ibid., 179.

PART THREE

BUILDING A FUNCTIONAL ORGANIZATION

CHAPTER SIX

FAREWELL TO CIRCULAR FIRING SQUADS

U p to this point, we have considered what to do with difficult individuals. Now in the second half of this book, we
turn to the even more daunting task of melding those individuals, quirky though they be, into a winning team.

It is embarrassing to admit that some of the conflicts we
have in business have nothing to do with employees' problems
—but rather with how we have organized them. In our institu-
tions we sometimes literally set people up to be enemies of each
other. We pit individuals against one another by the ways we
measure and reward. They end up almost like a firing squad in a
circle, aiming at one another, rather than in a straight line aiming at a common target.

When I walk into a business and find otherwise mature
people hiding information from each other, keeping secrets, and
making end runs, I know this is an unhealthy company. In some
organizations, I get the feeling that the person to beat is the person in the next office, not the real competitor across town. It
would be hard to overestimate the thousands of hours wasted in
many organizations as one individual or group seeks to succeed
at the expense of the other.

"For many people, the toughest competition and opposition

comes from internal rivals," Stephen R. Covey wrote in *Executive Excellence* magazine. He added, "In business, if you have dissension on your team, you won't be able to compete with world-class performers." Those who view their teammates as their fiercest opponents may feel too threatened to share power, knowledge, and inside information.

Maybe our educational system bred this into us long before we ever entered the workforce. On my first day of graduate school, the professor said, "Look at the person on your right and the person on your left. One of the three of you will not be here in six months; the other will be gone in a year. . . . By the way, I grade on the curve."

That's when I learned that my fellow students were not my teammates. I would be measured against them, and they against me. Meanwhile, none of us would really be measured on how much we had improved—only on whether we'd beaten the other fellow.

I wasn't surprised, therefore, when I found key books missing from the reference library. My "competitors" were not only using the books for their own term papers, but they were also keeping them from me.

In twenty-five years of public and private education, I never recall being given a team assignment—one where the final grade rested on how we worked together as a team. All learning, all research, all evaluations, all testing was highly individual—and highly competitive.

MISUSE OF DATA

Later on, when I became a corporate trainer, I was pleasantly surprised to discover the emphasis on team learning, case studies, peer coaching, pre- and post-testing (to chart improvement), and positive affirmation and reinforcement. I learned that progressive businesses do this because they understand the importance of teamwork. Smart managers know that few tasks can be accomplished by one individual working alone. Smart managers understand that their real task is not just to motivate superstars but to raise the performance level of the entire group.

However, many organizations in the United States today collect tons of data on human performance without knowing what to do with it. Performance data is useful only if you use it for one of the following:

- To fix a problem
- To make a decision
- To improve something

Otherwise, you're wasting your time. Actually, you could be doing something even worse—collecting data in order to blame someone. Employees refer to this as a "gotcha" system (and other terms that are not printable).

"Gotcha" systems are not uncommon. In fact, they are so common that most employees are leery of measurement of any kind, because yardsticks have been used as clubs to hit people over the head.

This is exactly what killed the concept known as Management by Objectives, or MBO, which was popular in the seventies. Some unsuspecting, sincere manager or associate would get enthused and set a high goal of a 10 percent increase. At the end of the year he or she would have a 7 percent improvement—no small accomplishment. Instead of being congratulated, however, this person would be criticized and even financially penalized for "failing" to meet the objective.

The second year he or she would set a much lower goal, and management would try to coax him to a higher one. By the third year the associate would catch on to the game and write a goal so vague that no one could ever measure it. Thus, what could have been an excellent management system degenerated into gobbledygook. Those who became really good at gobbledygook were promoted into executive positions.

In some cases this type of measurement degenerated into an approach that was downright silly. Once I was conducting a management seminar in New York, and a woman came bursting into the room late, looking somewhat flustered. At break time she rushed up to apologize.

"Dr. Stevenin, I'm so sorry I was late. You see, I had to get my MBOs turned in to Personnel this morning. We're already three months into the fiscal year, but I've been so busy and my staff has been so busy we just haven't had time to do them. So Personnel sent me a note on Friday that if I didn't have my MBOs in by this morning, I couldn't get my check. I had to spend the whole weekend doing my MBOs. I went by the office to give them to Personnel. Please excuse me."

I assured her that it was OK and welcomed her to the seminar. In the course of thirty seconds this well-intentioned manager had told me volumes about herself and her organization. Specifically:

- They had gotten through the first quarter without objectives.
- Therefore, a lot of work was going on that apparently had nothing to do with objectives.
- In this organization, a manager could write objectives at home without involving the people who had to implement them.
- The system was being driven by Payroll, not top management.
- The objectives were now secured in a file drawer in Personnel. I wondered what they would do with them.

Clearly, the whole process had degenerated into a paper chase with no relationship to reality. People are smart enough to know when this is true.

I'm not sure which is worse—using goals and measurements to punish people, or setting up a system of goals and measurements that is totally irrelevant to what is actually happening. Both approaches kill the inner spirit.

APPROACHES TO MEASUREMENT

In my view, there are three basic approaches to measuring what people do in the workplace. Two of them tend to create conflict. The third energizes the inner spirit and creates teamwork. Unfortunately, the first two are more common.

The Traditional Approach: Measure each individual's performance (or each group's performance) against a predetermined, fixed number or standard.

The Competitive Approach: Measure each individual's performance (or each group's performance) against other individuals or groups.

The Healthy Approach: Measure each individual's or each group's current level of performance against their own previous level of performance.

The strengths and weaknesses of these approaches are as follows:

Measuring against a fixed number or standard. This is so common that you may think me insane to challenge it. At the beginning of the year, most businesses set fixed goals for sales, profits, production, quality, market penetration, and costs. These are combined into the monthly and annual budget, which in turn drives everything else throughout the year.

Clearly, there are some advantages to this method. Businesses need a sense of where they are going financially. Lenders and investors also need to know. It's a fairly easy system to interpret: You either meet the goal or you don't. You succeed or you fail.

But therein lies the problem. *What looks like success can be failure.* Consider the following scenarios:

- An 82 percent first–run quality manufacturing operation sets a goal to get to 90 percent, and achieves it. Success? Not necessarily. A 10 percent reject rate is incredibly high. It may cost millions in rework and lost business. None of the real process problems may have been solved.
- A quality standard of 95 percent was set for two departments. In the most recent quarter they both made 96 percent. Therefore, they should be rewarded the same— right? Wrong. A year ago one department was at 99 percent but has been slowly deteriorating in quality. This problem needs to be analyzed. The other department has been steadily improving. This calls for celebration and reinforcement. The apparently identical situations are actually very different.
- A goal is set for a 14 percent increase in sales. Only 12 percent is achieved. This is a failure; bonuses cannot be paid in full, right? Wrong. A 12 percent increase is not a failure; it is a tremendous improvement. It must be positively rewarded and recognized.
- A goal of 90 percent attendance is established. Management really intends this to be a floor; in the minds of the workers, it becomes a ceiling. Performance tends to hover around this number, with employees thinking that it's best not to exceed this number by too much, or management will want to set a higher standard.
- A short–term profit goal may cause a company to avoid replacing worn equipment, training employees, or remodeling

the plant. The company is eating its own seed corn; it is sacrificing its own long-term future to achieve a short-term numerical goal. (Most airline companies are doing exactly this today.)

• A sales representative can earn a full bonus by achieving a fixed dollar amount of sales. Two months before the end of the year, she's already achieved her fixed target. She begins to store up orders for January. Why not? From the sales representative's viewpoint she (a) is not going to make a higher bonus for exceeding sales this year; (b) is keeping next year's goal lower; and (c) is off to a great start in January. The company, meanwhile, has lost a great opportunity to maximize profits.

There are real dangers in fixed numerical goals. Note this statement from Thomas Pyzdek, author of *An SPC Primer*:

The increasing attention to standards . . . is a step backwards. Virtually all of the great quality gurus—Juran, Deming, Crosby and many others—have expressed serious doubts about this approach. This is the first time I've ever seen a consensus among the gurus. Yet the quality systems standards have taken on a life of their own, and their influence continues to grow.[1]

Pyzdek also questions the direction the quality emphasis is taking.

Quality is a journey, not a destination. Unfortunately, . . . more and more managers are starting to think of quality as a static state. Thus, I am less enthusiastic about the direction of quality in the United States. Based solely on my gut feeling, it seems to me that there is an attitude among many U.S. business leaders that "Well, we've put that quality thing behind us. Let's get on to other things."[2]

Measuring employees or departments against each other. Americans love competition. Why not clearly rank groups or individuals against each other and give our greatest rewards to the most outstanding. What's wrong with that?

Actually, several things:

- A small number of winners versus a large number of losers cannot, by definition, be very motivating for a large number of people.
- People who need to work together as a team may be pitted against each other in an unhealthy way.
- In extreme cases, the folks at the bottom start plotting against the constant winners. They may even sabotage their equipment or find other ways to undermine them. We can all remember in school how the teacher's pet got pulverized during recess.
- The ranking system fails to show trends and improvement. My most improved sales representative may be at the bottom of the volume list. As a sales manager, I want to give my highest rewards to two types: those who consistently perform at a superb level, and those who show the greatest improvement over previous performance.

Measuring against one's own previous performance. The emphasis here is on improvement, not perfection. Deming often shocked us by insisting we do away with fixed standards as measurement. He understood both statistics and psychology. He knew that people never perform perfectly, but they can and do perform better. Helping people perform better is what great leaders do.

In this approach, our data system must clearly portray trends. All individuals and teams are either getting better, getting worse, or staying the same—those are the only three possibilities. The problem is that we rarely keep data on individuals or teams in a way that clearly portrays the trend.

Many businesses publish a weekly or monthly variance report, organized as follows:

Standard Goals   Actual Performance   Variances

When you pick up such a report, your eye immediately goes to the right side. No matter how well you are really doing, you focus on your failures.

Furthermore, the most important measurements aren't shown. What I really want to know as a manager is not how actual performance compares to standard, but how does actual performance last month compare to actual performance the previous month or the last six months. Are we getting better or worse or going nowhere?

SHOW POSITIVES, NOT NEGATIVES

If the greatest single thing leaders can do is reinforce improvement, then our measurement systems must focus on improvement. This is why I'm a great believer in graphs. Graphing human performance is a powerful form of feedback. However, such graphing should commend the positive, not point out the negative. What should we graph?

What to Graph	What Not to Graph
Attendance	Absenteeism
On-time work	Late work
Retention	Turnover
Percent of loans closed in five days	Percent of loans outside control limits
On-time shipments or reports	Late shipments or reports
Rooms cleaned perfectly	Rooms cleaned incorrectly

Putting a low performer's graph that shows improvement next to a high performer's may be punishing, rather than reinforcing. Instead of fostering higher goals and positive competition, it may create negative competition. Managers often aggravate this situation by cheering successful individuals and teasing lower performers. This increases the negative side effects of competition.

General Rule: *Publicly display group or team performance, and keep individual performance more private.* Avoid becoming overly dependent on your system. Systems don't give feedback or reinforcement. *People* use systems to make a positive impact on people.

SETTING UP A MEANINGFUL DATA SYSTEM

Frequently, a supervisor must modify data to make it useful to employees. For example, many people receive useless computer printouts every week or month, which must be modified to be significant. Data should be simplified and displayed graphically if possible.

Data-based systems also allow employees to monitor themselves, ultimately allowing the manager to do more true leading and less direct supervising. A data system is not a collection of gimmicks or motivating tricks, but an organized operating strategy for managers. It is a visual tracking of improvement.

Data-oriented approaches are integral to a high-performance workplace. The system focuses on changes and improvement, not personalities.

Why measure? Here are three strong reasons: (1) To reduce emotionalism and increase objectivity, constructive dialogue, and problem solving; (2) to increase the manager's influence over the things employees actually are doing; and (3) to reinforce progress, and provide feedback when progress is slow.

Managers may be reluctant to measure because it seems difficult and technical. Yet everything can be measured, usually in simple ways.

They may also hesitate because people have often encountered measurement as a prelude to punishment. They have yet to see a manager use measurement for good instead of bad.

FOUR THINGS TO MEASURE

What should you measure? Here are the four key areas:

1. *Quality.* Is the work meeting or exceeding an agreed-upon level of acceptability? What percent of accuracy is being achieved? Is it continually improving?
2. *Quantity.* How many acceptable products are produced? What is the trend?
3. *Timeliness.* How rapidly is acceptable work being completed? Are we on schedule? Ahead of schedule? Improving?
4. *Cost.* How much does the work cost to do? How much is being saved by doing it better? Are we doing it better?

These four measurements—*Quality, Quantity, Timeliness,* and *Cost* —need to be used in conjunction with performance goals.

WHAT IS THE BASELINE?

Collecting baseline performance data is one of the most important steps in any program. Some managers become so enthusiastic about launching the new program that they fail to take the extra time to gather baseline data beforehand.

Without baseline data, however, you'll never know if your

improvement system is successful. Baseline is what tells you how smart you were to do all this.

It also helps you to set priorities for the programs you want to implement. You can concentrate on those areas that have the greatest value to your organization.

After all, managers are in business to improve things. We all are reinforced when we see our operations make headway as a result of our efforts. And employees like to see their own improvements, too.

The best and easiest way to gather baseline data, obviously, is to analyze records of past performance: sales contacts, production, quality control, errors, inventory, shipments, etc. More commonly, however, what you want to know has never been documented before. In this case, you'll need to gather data on current performance before launching the new program.

The preceding paragraphs may seem so self-evident they're not worth mentioning. Don't believe it! Every day I see organizations launch multimillion dollar programs of formal training or team building or reengineering—without clarifying what they're trying to improve or setting up a healthy measurement system. Within weeks they have their workforce at each other's throats.

SEEING IS BELIEVING

As I've already said, graphs are a vital form of feedback. The recipient can quickly see what needs changing or improving—if the graph is well-designed. On the next page is a checklist to make sure that happens, "How to Measure Your Measurement System."

THE IMPROVEMENT-MINDED MANAGER

Meanwhile, what are the most important duties for a manager? While employees are busy learning how to improve, what is the best use of the manager's time and attention?

- Positively support the process.
- Give feedback to employees on specific behaviors.
- Analyze results with employees.
- Support changes for improvement.
- Coach employees for improvement.

How to Measure Your Measurement System	Yes	No
The graph is easy to understand.		
The graph contains no more than two lines of data.		
The graph is clearly labeled.		
The graph shows the baseline.		
The graph shows goals or standards as minimums.		
The graph shows improvements by an ascending line.		
The graph is set up to show appropriate variability in the data.		
The graph is attractive.		
The graph looks important.		
The graph is accessible to workers.		
The graph is kept up to date.		
The graph is maintained by those doing the work.		
The graph shows recent and current work.		
The graph relates only to things the employees can do.		
The graph shows a positive trend.		
The graph is used as a tool for feedback.		
The graph contains positive comments for improvements.		

- Focus attention on the graphs, so employees know graphs are important.
- Collect information and evaluate what is occurring.
- Set specific expectations.
- Stay open to new ideas; encourage creativity.

Each individual is always three persons. You and I are the private person we know ourselves to be. We are the public person seen by others as they view us in our official roles. But most of all, there is the dream, the picture in our minds of the more effective, more competent, more loving person we have the capacity to become. English Poet Laureate John Masefield called this person "the one he wanted to be."

Rather than pitting people against each other, organizations and their leaders must learn to nourish, encourage, and affirm improvement. We must help each person to become the person he or she dreams of being, for this is the person who will shape the future.

NOTES

1. As quoted in Scott Madison Patow, "New Gurus, The Next Leaders of the Quality Revolution," *Quality Digest* (March 1995), 36.
2. Ibid.

CHAPTER SEVEN

A SLIGHT
CHANGE
IN PLANS

The captain gave his soldiers the orders: "Ready. . . Fire . . . Aim." Quickly, the men carried out their leader's command. Standard orders, right? Wait. Go back and read the first paragraph again . . . slowly. It didn't read "Ready. . . Aim. . . Fire."

Ready . . . Fire! . . . Then, oops, guess I should have aimed. . . .

Blasting away at the inefficiencies and tensions of our organizations is not a good idea unless we first take time to zero in on our targets. Managers are infamous for taking action without proper forethought. We get too hurried.

In today's world, change has accelerated greatly. Change in the organization may be necessary, too. Yet change should not be automatic and rarely without much thought. Let's talk about proper approaches to change in our business.

Change is coming at us constantly from different directions and at constantly accelerating speeds.

Consider the advances in medicine. Only fifty years ago, there were no vaccines for polio or measles. No one outside a horror movie had ever attempted a heart transplant. We didn't even know the structure of a DNA molecule.

Fifty years ago, advanced technology had just created the long-playing record, which is now obsolete. Laser light was unknown then; now it plays our compact discs, the LP records of our time. A computer that used to occupy a whole room can now sit on your lap. And thanks to the Internet, it can connect you with people all over the world.

Satellite technology allows us to see the world on our televisions every day. And we've seen that world change radically. Whole countries have shifted boundaries—the two Germanys have become one, and the former communist Soviet Union has splintered into many countries struggling to become capitalist societies, which has opened new doors for international trade.

As the world becomes more globally oriented, we've learned to accommodate other cultures and lifestyles. Social, religious, and ethnic diversity abounds and is accepted. The traditional American family—in which the husband pursues a career and the wife works inside the home—has been joined by many two-career as well as single-parent households. White males, the former mainstay of the U.S. work force, now comprise only 47 percent of all workers. Experts predict that by the year 2000, white males will have dropped to a mere 12 percent of new hires. As the workforce becomes increasingly diverse, businesses must change the way they recruit and manage their employees.

All these changes can overwhelm us with their breadth, depth, and speed. In fact, such changes, and the rate at which they come, will flatten people and organizations who are not willing and prepared to deal with and capitalize on them.

This is not a time for Control Fanatics or Blamers. The self-absorbed behaviors that we outlined in the first two chapters just are not going to be usable in the twenty-first century. We must learn to guide people toward the bigger picture, leaving behind their selfish agendas so they can concentrate on improvement and productivity.

WHAT WE KNOW ABOUT CHANGE

On an intellectual level, we affirm that change has been with us always, is with us today, and will be with us for every tomorrow we'll ever know. That means we need to adapt to change with as little damage as possible.

You might reasonably think that the more change a person has gone through in life, the less frightening it becomes, the better he is at dealing with it, and the more he welcomes and enjoys future changes.

Think again.

As Mark Twain put it more than a century ago, "The only person who likes change is a wet baby."

Each day I deal with bright leaders who still have feelings of trepidation and anxiety, if not outright fear, of change. I understand why. All change involves some loss, if only the loss of comfort that comes from doing things the way we have always done them. Resistance is simply evidence that people are highly committed to the way things are.

William Sandy comments:

> There is a lot of pain for people when they try to change from something familiar to something new and different. Managers often fail to appreciate that people who have not accepted or "bought into" the vision will continue to see things as they are, not as they are going to be.
>
> A construction site, for example, is a mess of destruction for a while, but that's the reason for the architect's sketch. It portrays the vision of the fine new facility that will emerge from the chaos.
>
> That's important, because a lot of people get frustrated by upheaval. They need to be reminded that changes in method are the business parallel to all the banging, clanging, dirt, and confusion of a construction site, something worth going through to accomplish something better.[1]

Changes in the workplace are particularly discomforting in today's climate of corporate downsizing. Workers desperate to hang on to their jobs seldom welcome the uncertainty that change brings and the effects it has on relationships. No matter what the reason for restructuring, whenever personnel holes appear in an organization, personal relationships develop holes as well.

Sadly, so much time is spent creating the new wheel that little time is left to consider the people in its path and how it will roll over them. Most leaders do a woefully inadequate job of preparing people for change. Managers who are well prepared to deal with the nuts and bolts of the change process can be ill prepared to deal with the human ruts and revolts. Consequently, as managers organize and implement change, the human side often gets undermanaged.

A good leader must recognize employees' fear of change and help them overcome it, promoting the change for the good of the company. Managers who organize and implement the change have an essential role: to keep the lines of communication open, ensuring that information is shared among all levels of the organization. Managers must help employees overcome their resistance to the change, maintain their confidence, and continue to be productive throughout the transition.

If anything, overcommunicate. I've never known a leader to get into trouble by overcommunicating.

FEELINGS ABOUT CHANGE

Because change destroys the status quo, it naturally results in insecurity. As the comfort level drops or disappears, the void is filled with uncertainty. "Who am I changing all this for?" "What do I do now?" "Where do I fit in?" "When will this all make sense—if ever?" "Why me?" "How will I ever be able to get my job done with a new organizational structure?"

Two experts point out that when a company undergoes a significant change such as restructuring, employees often experience a grief process similar to losing a loved one. The stages of the grief process are: (1) shock and denial, (2) anger, (3) hurt, (4) inadequacy, (5) fear, (6) guilt, and (7) depression. Physical symptoms may occur; the final stage is acceptance.[2]

If changes aren't handled effectively by managers, creativity, productivity, and innovation can become casualties. Employees who don't understand and agree with the changes may become disillusioned, skeptical, angry, and fearful. They turn into Stealthy Stalkers or even sometimes into Sherman Tanks.

People fear and resist change for a variety of reasons. People with a poor self-image lack the confidence to believe that they can, in fact, effectively meet the coming changes. When organizational change is solely due to downsizing, even survivors can be left with uncertainty. They fear they will be the next to go.

Some people resist change because they think there is only one way to do things: the way they have been done in the past. Others are more leery than fearful, doubting the company is sincere or that the proposed change will in fact work the wonders it proposes. Those simply willing to wait out a change will adopt the attitude "If I close my eyes, everything will go away." And indeed, everything might.

In several situations, change makes conflict likely. Key reasons for the conflict are: (1) The reasons for the change are unclear; (2) employees were not involved in the planning; or (3) communication is poor. Change also will increase conflict if:

- The change does not fit the employee's values, beliefs, and goals.
- The reward does not appear to be worth the cost.
- There's not enough time to prepare people.
- The employee fears there is no room for failure while learning.
- The employee lacks confidence in his or her ability.
- The employee thinks the organization is not behind the change.
- The employee thinks all things pass and so will this.
- There's a desire to continue as is.
- There's a lack of trust.
- The employee is already under too much stress.

ASSESSING YOUR READINESS FOR CHANGE

To determine whether your company is ready for a change, consider the following factors:

Motivation. Does management project a strong sense of urgency that is shared by the rest of the company? Does the company already emphasize continuous improvement? Change is more difficult in a corporate culture that discourages risk-taking.

Vision. How clear is management's picture of the future? In order to work together effectively, team members must have a clear sense of the company's vision and goals. Managers should help team members stay focused on the corporate direction and work for the rewards that vision can offer.

People need to see and understand why fearing, fighting, and fending off change freezes their energies or redirects them in nonproductive ways.

Criteria for measurement. Does your company use performance measures of the sort encouraged by total quality management (acceptability rates, time-to-market, etc.) that express the economics of the business? Are compensation and reward systems used to reinforce these measures? They should be.

Organization structure. The best situation is a fluid, flexible organization in which major reorganizations are rarely needed. To be most efficient in the new scheme of things, you will need flexibility. During the course of change, efficiency may dictate that you perform some duties formerly handled elsewhere, such as preparing a FedEx package yourself instead of sending it off to the shipping department.

Processes. How willing are executives (and the organization as a whole) to change critical processes and sacrifice perks or power for the good of the group? Major changes almost invariably require redesigning business processes that cut across functions such as purchasing, accounts payable, or marketing. Rigidly turf-conscious executives make change more difficult.

Competitors. Does your organization compare its performance with competitors and systematically examine changes in the market? It should.

Client focus. The customer is extremely important. She or he should be the focal point of any major change in organization. Placing the attention anywhere else is akin to rearranging deck chairs on a sinking ship. The more everyone in the company focuses on customers, the more likely that the organization can agree to change to serve them better.

It can no longer be management beating labor, or labor beating management. It must be management and labor working together to provide the best possible service to the customer.

Rewards. Change is easier if managers and employees are rewarded for taking risks, being innovative, and looking for new solutions. Team-based rewards are better than individual rewards.

Managers should break the ice and let employees know that they understand that change is stressful for them. I know of one company that brought in a dunking booth and allowed employees to pelt the bosses with water balloons for putting them through this change. Or perhaps you could hire a fund-raising organization to wash every car in the lot. Show that you're a good sport, and realize what you're asking of the employees. Let them know that you appreciate their efforts and that you believe everyone will ultimately benefit from the change.

Diversity. Does your company employ people of both sexes and from a variety of ethnic backgrounds? Organizations that successfully manage diversity are more likely to be effective in coping with change, because diversity generates multiple perspectives on business problems and opportunities.

Communication. Does your company have two-way communication that reaches all levels and that all employees use and understand? If so, it will adapt to change better than a company in which most communication is from the top down.

Innovation. Does your company experiment? Are new ideas implemented fairly easily? Do employees work across internal boundaries with little trouble? If so, change will be easier than in a company with lots of channels and red tape.

DON'T CHANGE EVERYTHING

According to Stanford University professors James Collins and Jerry Porras, companies must evolve—but not change everything—and this is where a leader can make all the difference. It's one thing to alter a company's systems and methods, but quite another to tinker too much with the very core.

"Everything is up for change in an organization, except the core ideology," says Porras. Drawing on their observations of eighteen long-lasting companies and interviews with chief executives, Porras and Collins say the values and philosophies held by the corporate leaders remain key to the psychic focus of a company. They describe this as one of two critical aspects of a company, the other being its operations. In other words, there's what the company does, and there is its soul.[3]

Values are defined by Webster's Dictionary as "a principle standard or quality considered inherently worthwhile or desirable." The root for value is *valor,* which means strength. Values are sources of strength, because they give people the power to take action. Values are deep and emotional and often difficult to change —as they should be.

Values are the essence of a company's philosophy for achieving success. They are the bedrock of corporate culture. Values provide employees with a sense of common direction and guidelines for day-to-day behavior. Max DePree in his classic book *Leadership Is an Art* says:

Leadership [is] liberating people to do what is required of them in the most effective and most human way possible... Leadership is more tribal than scientific, more a weaving of relationships than amassing information.[4]

Those human values begin with leaders, writes James O'Toole of the USC Graduate School of Business:

Leaders must be clear about their own beliefs—have thought through their assumptions about human nature—the role of the organization and how to measure performance.[5]

A person's values answer the question "What's important to me?" Our values are the deep-seated pervasive standards that influence almost every aspect of our lives: our moral judgments, our responses to others, our commitments to personal and organizational goals. We all have belief systems we live by. Our beliefs and value systems are deeply connected. We are motivated and make decisions based on these belief systems and values. Often these values are unconscious.

If we all had the same values with the same priorities, it would be easy to work in groups. Most teams, however, have a diversity of values and beliefs. To help us work better as a team and make decisions that lead to commitment and action, it is necessary to see the range of values that influence the decision-making process and find ways to prioritize and clarify the values used.

EXAMPLES OF TEAM VALUE STATEMENTS

A faculty group in a medical center evolved the following statement to represent the underlying values on which they designed their training program for nurse practitioners and physician assistants.

- The means are not separate from the ends in the practice of health care.
- Self-care, self-awareness, and self-referenced behavior are essential practices for educators in order to teach these skills to our students.
- Relationships with our patients are focused on assisting them to return to a state of physical, mental, and emotional well-being.

- The real art of health care is based on the humanistic application of scientific knowledge.
- A desire to reemphasize the importance of attitudinal, interpersonal, and self-care issues is necessary in the education of health professionals.
- The task of educators is to provide the best possible technical training along with the transmission and articulation of ideas and values.

Robert Haas, chairman and CEO of Levi Strauss, has said: "We've learned. . . that the soft stuff and the hard stuff are becoming increasingly intertwined. A company's values—what it stands for, what its people believe in—are crucial to its competitive success. Indeed, values drive the business."[6]

Change is easier for a company in which decisions are based on clear values.

PREPARING PEOPLE FOR CHANGE

How you announce a change affects employees' reaction to it. Begin by describing the change in detail. Give background information and explain why the change is necessary. Be clear about how the change will affect employees.

Next, ask employees to describe the difficulties associated with the change. Be open to questions and explore together what it means and how they feel.

Assign difficulties to specific teams for problem solving. Let all employees know that their involvement is important and that their input will affect how the change is carried out.

Ask each person to identify one or more potential personal benefits he or she will derive from the change in the next six to twenty-four months. Also ask each person to identify potential benefits to the organization.

As previously noted, resistance to change is understandable and natural. In fact, resistance is usually evidence that people have a high level of commitment to the way things have been effectively done in the past—which is as it should be. However, as Thomas Holcraft once put it, "The past is a guidepost . . . not a hitching post."

To unhitch employees from their past and free them to ride toward some future mind-set, the first task of management is to discern and accept the reason for the resistance. Managers should make it safe to express resistance and probe to uncover what the employee doesn't like about the change. Have the employee explore the resistance by stating it in specific terms. Help employees identify the positive aspects of the change, and let them know you will support them throughout the transition.

Once the manager understands the resistance, he or she must diffuse and redirect the force of that resistance through the five R's of change.

Reality. Tell the truth. Give honest background information about why the change is necessary. Don't apologize if the sole purpose is to be more cost-effective or profitable. In the long run, employees are hurt by unprofitable companies, not profitable ones. This observation was first made by Samuel Gompers, founder of the American labor movement. However painful or ugly the information may be, people respect being told the truth.

Furthermore, when dealt with honestly, they feel respected. Never promise what you can't deliver. Don't say, "None of you will be negatively affected by this." You can't guarantee that.

Responsibility. Ultimately, it is everyone's responsibility to make a change become effective as best he can. However, it is the responsibility of effective managers to lead the way into the new environment and to bring those on your team right along with you. Try to express as clearly as possible how you expect the change to affect your employees.

People adamant in the belief that "if it ain't broke, don't fix it" will need to be shown breaks that currently exist and any foreseeable future breakdowns. These may be impending changes in markets or market shares, changes in resources or resource availability, or technology.

Explaining the specific reasons for the change shows that proactive rather than reactive ideas are at work. This makes the reward appear to be worth the cost. Perhaps investing in recycling technology or a faster computer system would then be seen as a good move. Adjusting to a business-related inevitability shows that the company is stretching to stay competitive rather than changing simply for the sake of change.

Proactive managers look for opportunities to stretch their employees and show faith in their willingness and ability to stay on the cutting edge.

Relationships. As you probe the causes of any resistance that does exist, capitalize on good relationships and let employees know they are valued contributors. Listen, respond, and reframe their concerns, opinions, and suggestions.

People need to know that their input is valued and that their involvement is important to you, to the success of the change, and to the future of the company. Make it safe to express resistance and fear. Accept those feelings as normal and natural. Never belittle their apprehension. Assure them that there is room for failure while learning. This approach will not only help people stretch but will help solidify what they learn from one of the greatest teachers of all: mistakes.

A sure cause of resistance to change is leaving employees out of the planning. To counteract that, be open to questions. Explore together what the change will mean and how people are feeling about it. All the while, look to implement good suggestions for smoother transitions. Such suggestions will likely come out of open discussions—never out of no discussions. You won't get suggestions if the only question you ask is: "Do you want to keep your job, or don't you?"

Renewal. This comes from feeling the combined commitments of the organization, the immediate team, and the individual team members. It evolves through a normal period of uncertainty and apprehension. Remember that at some point any major organizational or strategic change will appear to be a failure. The good leader has the courage to move the organization through the uncomfortable period to the ultimate triumph.

No matter how well you prepare for change, some conflicts will arise. People have short memories. They quickly forget how bad the old system was. Two individuals will always emerge at this point. The Negaholic predicts gloom and doom and insists that disaster is about to occur. The other person insists that this will be the organization's finest hour.

Results. Our firm has worked closely with the Harley–Davidson Motor Company of Milwaukee and their outstanding training program known as Harley–Davidson University. A few years ago Harley was near bankruptcy, supplied only 15 percent of the American motorcycle market, and had a poor reputation for quality. New leadership led the organization into a wrenching reengineering process focused on teams and quality processes. Today,

Harley-Davidson supplies 80 percent of the American market and is rapidly expanding in Europe. You have to be on a waiting list for six to eighteen months to buy a new motorcycle. The price of change is high; the payoff is even higher.

LEADERS MUST EXHIBIT
GREAT COURAGE AND FAITH

The great Jewish leader Moses must have been astonished when the people of Israel, in the midst of their exhilarating march toward freedom and nationhood, announced they wanted to go back to Egypt and make bricks without straw as slaves to the Pharaoh. But Moses rose to the occasion. He pushed, pulled, and prayed his people through the wilderness to the Promised Land.

I used to wonder why Jesus of Nazareth began so many of His teachings with the words "You don't have to be afraid." Jesus was building a leadership team that would found the world's largest and longest enduring organization, the Church. By the time the lives of these unlikely, uneducated, blue-collar nobodies were finished, history would be divided B.C. and A.D. The message of hope and salvation would spread throughout the world.

Jesus was preparing His followers for change, changed values, changed lives, and changes in the inner person (where all lasting change occurs). He understood He had a lot of preparing to do.

Change is not your organization's enemy. It is, with proper handling, your ticket to a healthy future.

NOTES

1. William Sandy, *Forging the Productivity Partnership* (New York: McGraw-Hill, 1994), 23.
2. Cited in Thomas Holcraft, *Equipping Managers for Change* (Atlanta: Resource Associates, 1988).
3. "James Collins and Jerry Porras,"*Profiles* magazine, February 1996, 32.
4. Max DePree, *Leadership Is an Art* (New York: Dell, 1990), 1, 3.
5. Ibid., xix.
6. Robert Haas, unpublished speech.

CHAPTER EIGHT

THE GOOD SIDE OF CONFLICT

Let's take a look at some prevalent conceptions about conflict:
"Conflict is morally wrong (a sin) and requires apology and forgiveness."

"Conflict destroys organizations."

"Conflict destroys interpersonal relationships (including marriages)."

"Conflict prevents good decision making."

"Conflict is abnormal."

"Conflict has no place in a working environment."

"Conflict inhibits productivity."

"Conflict should be eliminated by good leaders."

All of these statements have one thing in common: They are false! Worse, they are misleading.

Conflict is a basic, necessary ingredient of all healthy human relationships, including marriages, and is present in all walks of organizational life, especially the workplace. The only place you'll find a large group of human beings coexisting perfectly without conflict is a cemetery. Any working environment that prohibits conflicting opinions is a dictatorship.

A relationship devoid of conflict is superficial, hollow, and so polite that it seldom leads to innovation or dynamic progress.

Eventually it results in poor decision making and boredom. The contribution of such a relationship to the workplace is almost negligible, since it demotes a thinking, creative human being to a submissive and often resentful automaton.

How often have I heard these lines?

"Conflict doesn't exist in our organization." This is nothing less than total denial, and is a mire that can bog one down indefinitely. To deny such a stark reality in your daily affairs is nothing short of irrational and will inevitably slow or stop progress in the business at hand.

Why do people pretend a painful situation isn't bothering them? When I've asked that question to women and men in a variety of jobs and professions, here are some of the responses I've received:

"I can't do anything about it, so I just swallow my pride and put up with it."

"It goes with the territory."

"It's only a job."

"It's only money."

"It's not worth taking personally."

No matter the response, they cannot readily ignore conflict. Conflict does exist, because people have different opinions and will disagree.

"Conflict should be avoided." This is the peace-at-any-price mentality. It quickly becomes a treadmill of apathy or emotional suppression. This approach often results from the misconception that all conflict is "fighting," with the accompanying moral implications.

"Conflict is sin." This lays a heavy load of irrational guilt on an organizational leader. Such feelings usually require us to back off from our own suggestions. They can seriously deteriorate our own feelings of self-worth.

It is *not* a sin to espouse ideas that may conflict with those of others. It is more likely to be a sin of omission to remain silent when you have something useful to add.

"Conflict means we're doing something wrong." This is a combination of the above scenarios. It leads us to see ourselves as peacekeepers, offering emotional gratification. But once again, nothing really gets accomplished, and we usually end up feeling even more guilty in the process.

None of these approaches is conducive to a good working relationship in any setting. They serve only to cut us out of the decision-making process. They are uniformly ineffective and unproductive. Worst of all, such ideas make it impossible for us to retain our identity and self-esteem.

GO AHEAD, ROCK THE BOAT

Why is it that so many people do not really confront issues directly and constructively? I think there are a number of reasons.

First of all, dealing with anger constructively is often more uncomfortable at first than dealing with it destructively. It takes time and effort to deal with anger in a positive way, especially when first learning how.

Second, many people have been taught that standing up to others is wrong. They have gotten the impression that nice, compliant, religious people accept things meekly. They may get so much praise for being such a "nice" person that they find it very hard to confront.

In his book *Free for the Taking*, missionary Joseph Cooke tells how he tried to suppress his anger:

> I remember that for years and years of my life, I worked to bring my emotions under control. Over and over again, as they cropped up, I would master them in my attempt to achieve what looked like a gracious, imperturbable Christian spirit. Eventually, I had everybody fooled, even in a measure my own wife. But it was all a fake. I had a nice-looking outward appearance; but inside, there was almost nothing there. . . .
>
> And way underneath, almost completely beyond the reach of my subconscious mind, the mass of feelings lay bottled up. I didn't even know they were there myself, except when their pale ghosts would surface now and then in various kinds of unsanctified attitudes and reactions. But they were there nevertheless. And the time came when the whole works blew up in my face, in an emotional breakdown.
>
> All the things that had been buried so long came out in the open. Frankly, there was no healing, no recovery, no building a new life for me until all those feelings were sorted out, and until I learned to know them for what they were, accept them, and find some way of expressing them honestly and nondestructively.[1]

It is also a fact of life that the people who are closest to you are those most likely to anger you. You have the most interchange with them, and you hold the highest expectations.

Expect to get angry at people who are close to you! It is, in fact, normal. It is a part of life, if you care deeply about certain matters and each other.

When we express our honest feelings in constructive ways, true love is never killed but strengthened. Expressing anger constructively will never damage a worthwhile relationship. If a relationship is destroyed by attempting to deal constructively with angry feelings, it was probably a sick relationship to start with. Not much was lost.

This is interpersonal communication at its best. It reflects caring. It signifies that I want to stay in a respectful relationship with you, and I want you to know where I stand and what I am feeling, needing, valuing, and wanting. I want to know the same about you. These are the two arms of genuine relationship: confrontation with the truth; affirmation with love.

Otherwise, you end up papering over the conflict. How many of these expressions have you used recently?

- Status quo—"Don't rock the boat."
- Schmoozing—"Don't be negative. Emphasize the positive. We're a team, right?"
- Patriarchal/matriarchal—"When you've been around here as long as I have, you'll understand that . . ."
- Stalemate—"Let's just agree to disagree."
- Negotiation—"Let's meet each other halfway."
- Concession—"To get along, you have to go along."
- False support—"I don't really agree, but go ahead and give it a try."
- Postponement—"Let's talk about it later."

SOME CONSEQUENCES OF UNRESOLVED CONFLICT

A conflict left unresolved can damage both the work environment and the personalities. Even a resolution attempt that seems doomed to fail is better than no attempt at all, because at least a manager can exert some influence over the fallout. It's worthwhile to address the conflict. Otherwise, you are stuck with such things as:

- The loss of technically skilled and valuable employees who "just can't get along." They may resign, you may have to reassign them, or in the worst cases, you may have to dismiss them.
- The withholding or distorting of information that sincere coworkers need to continue performing.
- Poorer decisions by individuals and teams because they're busy focusing on personalities instead of problems.
- Possible sabotage of work or equipment. This is usually excused as "an accident" or "forgetfulness." The expense, however, can be monstrous.
- Sabotage of personal relationships and the reputations of team members through gossip and rumors. Once a person's focus falls upon emotional and personal issues instead of organizational goals, it tends to stay there.
- Dampened morale, enthusiasm, and job motivation. One resentful worker who feels wronged can quickly poison an entire team. Enthusiasm, once dampened, can prove very difficult for a manager to revive.
- Stress–related problems. These range from reduced efficiency to absenteeism.

KINDS OF CONFLICT

So we must wade in. Regardless of all the precautions we take, once we're involved, conflict can and will get ugly at times! Conflict often takes on varying styles:

1. *Simple problem solving.* Here the focus is on solutions to present problems; personalities do not gain priority as an issue.
2. *Accommodation/compromise.* Both parties are willing to give and take; however, real issues are not always addressed directly. Be on the lookout for emotional issues that never come to the table. Sometimes all parties remain dissatisfied.
3. *Disagreement.* This level of conflict is characterized by polarized opinions. Lines are drawn. As a leader, you want to

harness and direct the healthy aspects of disagreement without allowing the group to divide across rigid battle lines.

4. *Win/lose.* This is disagreement with a highly competitive attitude thrown in. At this level, people often show little regard for the opinions and ideas of others. Some will use any technique necessary to win the fight.

5. *Fight/flight.* This is the "sniper's" conflict. Participants take potshots at one another and then retreat to safety. As tempers flare, emotions overpower reason. Personalities clash.

6. *Intractable.* This is the "my way or no way" mentality. The only saving grace of this conflict is that it usually holds fast to logical lines of thought. However, there is no flexibility, and thus no resolution.

7. *Denial.* This is one of the most difficult types of conflict to deal with, because there is no open, frank communication. Conflict has gone underground. A conflict that cannot even be addressed is one without a solution.

HOW DID WE GET INTO THIS MESS?

Ray Pneuman of the Alban Institute in Washington, D.C., identifies the following common sources of conflict:

- People hold very different values and beliefs.
- The organization's structure is unclear.
- The leader's roles and responsibilities are not carefully spelled out.
- The organization has outgrown its structure.
- Leadership and membership styles don't mix well.
- A new leader rushes into change.
- Communication lines are blocked.
- The leader does not anticipate conflict—does not understand that conflict is inevitable.
- Disaffected followers hold back participation and support.
- A new leader tries to follow one with long tenure who was held in high esteem.

FIVE STEPS TO PEACE

Whatever the source of the problem, the following five steps are fundamental in working through the difficulty:

1. *Recognition.* Here you identify the gap between how things are and how things should be. The only pitfalls are errors in detection (overlooking a problem, or seeing a problem where none exists).
2. *Diagnosis.* This is the most important of the five steps. The tried and true method of *who, what, why, where,* and *how* works perfectly. Be careful to focus on primary matters, not trivia.
3. *Agreeing on solutions.* Gather input from all participants on possible solutions. Screen out the least viable or practical. Never settle for second best. Go for the gold.
4. *Implementation.* Keep in mind that there will be losses and gains. Be careful not to let such considerations overly af-fect the group's choices and course.
5. *Evaluation.* Solutions can of themselves generate an entire-ly new set of problems. If the solution doesn't seem to be working, go back through the previous steps and try it again.

As you apply these five steps to peace, keep in mind the need to involve everyone, even as you lead. How do you achieve a win/win solution? Here are some practical tips from conflict management specialist Herbert Kindler:

1. *Don't impose a solution.* A collective view must emerge nei-ther from coercion or majority vote, but from forthright, empathetic discussion.
2. *Provide background information.* Stakeholders must present their views with enough background for others to see them in context. Say what really matters to you, including your assumptions, hopes and fears.
3. *Don't surrender your view to reduce group tension.* If you throw in the towel to be a "nice guy" or to avoid the heat of con-frontation, you deny others the benefit of your insights and reasoning. You probably won't feel committed to whatever is decided.

4. *Actively invite different views.* This is not a win–lose competition. Everyone can win, but only when the richness of diverse views are honestly expressed and then creatively blended.

5. *Search deeply for understanding.* Listen to others respectfully to appreciate their insights. Honor their disclosures as you would a valued gift. Allow some time for silent reflection. Test your understanding with the speaker on complex issues.

6. *Keep testing ideas for group acceptance.* As you integrate ideas, keep checking to determine when relevant interests are satisfied and concerns adequately addressed.[2]

Kindler gives several additional tips on *concluding* an agreement in his book *Managing Disagreement Constructively:*

1. *Document your agreement.* Even personal agreements between parents and children are more effective when written. A carefully typed statement demonstrates commitment and provides a reference for the future when memories get hazy.

2. *Draft your agreement as discussions progress.* As you search for how to phrase your agreement, the intentions of both parties will be clarified. Participants also will see what issues, terms and conditions remain on the agenda to be resolved.

3. *Decide how results will be monitored.* What will be measured? How? By whom? For how long? What will constitute a successful outcome? Get commitments from individuals for deadlines for completing specific responsibilities.

4. *Discuss what happens if . . .* A big "if" to consider is the possibility of nonperformance. Whether you are drafting a legally binding contract or simply jotting a note to tape on the refrigerator door, the *consequences* of not living up to the agreement should be clear in advance.

5. *Help the other person sell the agreement "back home."* Determine if your disputant needs further approval or ratification. If so, strengthen his or her hand by rehearsing arguments that might persuade others to go along.

6. *Set a realistic deadline.* Is timely closure important to you? If so, indicate why. Perhaps if you don't resolve your differ-

ences by next Tuesday, you can't guarantee delivery, or hold the interest rate, or assure approval. Deadlines stir action.[3]

GUIDELINES FOR RESOLVING CONFLICT

As you read the above recommendations, you are no doubt thinking about all the little things that can go wrong along the way. The Five Steps to Peace make perfect sense . . . but what if a Rambo blows up in the middle of the meeting? What if one of the other Sherman Tanks starts revving his engine for a counter-charge?

Before you begin, consider the setting. *Create a safe, secure atmosphere.* When people feel comfortable, they will honestly voice their opinions. You can achieve a secure atmosphere not only by your tone and choice of terms, but even by the seating arrangement. It's easy to compete across a table but more difficult when sitting next to one another or in a circle.

An informal setting with a clearly defined agenda assists greatly in this. If you are the leader, remain vulnerable to criticism yourself. Make sure this is understood by all.

Here are some other ideas for guiding the process of conflict resolution:

- Be a stickler on facts. Quickly define the generalizations that crop up at this stage, such as "never" and "always." These broad terminologies are usually less than accurate.
- Involve everyone. Many managers attempt to carry this burden alone, which undermines equal responsibility.
- Keep the focus on a win/win solution for those involved. Emphasize points of mutual agreement instead of points of dispute.
- Give your team space and time to get where they are going. If forced or pressed into an agreement, resentments will be redirected to you.

Even following these guidelines does not assure that those involved are truly dealing with their disagreements. Any of the following actions (or inactions) tell you that parties are sidestepping potential conflict:

- Unwillingness to discuss anything except "safe" topics
- Premature agreement just to "keep the peace"
- Letting others carry the ball
- Silence from usually talkative members
- Failure to move on to the next logical steps
- Unwillingness to share information
- Knowing glances and nonverbal cues
- Recycling of old ideas

THE LEADER'S ROLE

Conflicts often arise in a vacuum of leadership. Think about your staff and your regular meetings. During those times, you should be conveying hope and optimism. You should communicate that whatever the problem or conflict, it *is* manageable. In addition, you should effectively express a sincere concern for everyone's success and that resolving conflicts will help, not hurt, people. During regular meetings, really listen to your team, separating facts from opinions and feelings.

As you prepare to meet, ask yourself these questions:

- Have I established some ground rules? three basic ones are (1) put-downs are not allowed; (2) there is no punishment for being honest; and (3) all feelings are acceptable.
- Have I communicated that all involved are needed?
- Do I communicate that I care about you?
- Do I communicate that I care about our relationship?
- Do I communicate that I care about this company?
- Do I communicate that I want you to have some real input in how this will be resolved?

SOME CONFLICT DON'TS

As you deal with conflict, take care to avoid these don'ts. First, *don't get drawn into a power struggle with others.* An established maxim of sociology is that authority increases as power decreases, and vice versa. You can enhance, not detract from, your authority as a manager by giving away power to others on your team, which also establishes trust and respect. This also helps to deter employees from jockeying for power.

On the other extreme, *don't become overly detached from the conflict*. The dynamics and outcome of any conflict can be best managed from inside.

Also, *don't let your vision be established by the conflict at hand*. Keep your managerial perspective by concentrating on the important issues. Your most immediate problem is not necessarily your greatest opportunity.

Conflict, when mixed with anger and personal attack, can become evil and ugly. It can divide and destroy marriages and organizations, or indeed almost any relationship. Unharnessed, it can lead to divorce, abuse, termination, one-upmanship, manipulation, and a host of other social ills, each with potentially dire consequences for the combatants.

But conflict is not necessarily combat. Combat, whether verbal or physical, exists when two people who need to work together are attacking each other in rage and bitterness. Such behavior disrupts work, paralyzes problem solving, and poisons morale. The critical difference between combat and conflict is anger and how it is used.

Conflict should be dealt with quickly, but it does not always have to be dealt with immediately. There's nothing wrong with saying, "What you said did upset me, but I'll have to think it through before I say anything more about it." Or you might tag the situation by saying, "Something about that bothers me, but it's not clear to me yet. Maybe when I've had a chance to think it over we can talk about it." Tagging the situation marks it as a problem to you and the other person, but you are consciously deferring any definitive action. It also alerts the other person to think about what was said and done, decreasing the chance that he will forget about it.

Whenever possible, do your confronting in private. If a problem has developed between you and another individual, endeavor to resolve it between the two of you alone, without involving others. As the ancient wisdom of Proverbs says, "Do not go out hastily to argue your case; otherwise what will you do in the end, when your neighbor puts you to shame? Argue your case with your neighbor, and do not reveal the secret of another."[4]

ASCRIBING MOTIVES

One habit that always turns a conflict ugly is to ascribe

motives to an opponent. We never ascribe good motives, of course—only those that make our opponent seem narrow, self-seeking, vengeful, or stupid.

Thus we too easily create a monster from the cloth of our own insecurities. No manager, for example, will ever get beyond his anxiousness as long as he believes that every question and objection is a challenge to his authority.

Once we have stripped the difficult person of all positive qualities, we commit further aggression by building consensus against the individual. We air our grievances to any and all who will hear. We ask others about their experience with the terrible individual, with the strong implication that we want to hear "the dirt."

The result of this amateur group therapy, unfortunately, is that we become more convinced than ever of the justice and wisdom of our negativism. How could we be wrong with so many coworkers affirming our outrage?

In the final analysis, serious conflict can only be resolved by confrontation. Here is where I have had my greatest struggles. I dislike confronting. I postpone it too long.

I have learned a great deal from David Augsburger's book *Caring Enough to Confront*. He says, "Avoiding honest statements of real feelings and viewpoints is often considered kindness, thoughtfulness, or generosity. More often it is the most cruel thing I can do to others. It is a kind of benevolent lying."[5]

He draws a distinction between "I Feel" and "Blaming You" messages. Here are examples of the two kinds of messages:

Two Kinds of Conflict Messages

"I Feel"	"Blaming You"
I'm feeling ignored.	You're making me mad because you're paying so much attention to Mary.
I feel disappointed that I can't go too.	You're making me angry by deliberately leaving me behind.
I get the feeling that I'm being blamed for that.	You always blame me for everything that goes wrong.
I feel put down.	You're always putting me down.
I feel like I'm being interrogated.	Why are you finding fault with me again?

"I Feel" messages keep communication open, while "Blaming You" messages put the other person on the defensive and restrict further communication.

DEALING WITH YOUR FEELINGS

Some people are afraid of confronting someone because they don't know if they will be able to control their anger. For most people, learning to confront others is very uncomfortable at first. But despite the disconcerting feelings, very few people end up physically or verbally attacking the other person if they have thought through the steps listed previously.

However, if someone feels violently angry, he may have to put off confrontation and get some help, perhaps even professional help, so that he will eventually be able to confront the person without losing control.

To deal well with your feelings, keep in mind these suggestions as you confront:

- Be professional and managerial, even if the other person gets petty or nasty.
- Be specific and constructive, pointing out exactly what this person did that was misleading or dishonest, and what you will need in the future in order to trust this person again and work well together.
- Be prepared for this person to argue, disagree, lie, or manipulate without your having to get defensive or upset. Just repeat what you found to be unacceptable behavior and what you would prefer in the future.
- Don't try to transform or "fix" this individual. He or she has picked up bad habits for reasons that have little to do with you.
- Don't expect overnight changes. It may take five or ten direct conversations before this person realizes you are not being swayed and that manipulation doesn't work with you.
- Don't wait too long to bring up the problem. The longer you wait, the more this person will think that his or her tactics are working on you.

FOCUS ON OBJECTIVE BEHAVIOR

Rather than focusing on an individual's attitude (subjective), it is more constructive to focus on the person's behavior (objective).

Imagine that a member of your team comes to the meeting and sits with arms folded for the first ten minutes. He then takes out a newspaper and starts to work on a crossword puzzle. A few minutes later he starts whispering to his neighbor. Ten minutes later he gets up to go make a phone call.

How might we describe this person's behavior?

We might say he has a bad attitude, does not care about the team's objectives, lacks enthusiasm—or we might simply call him impolite. Can you imagine trying to change this person's attitude? It would be very difficult.

What we *can* change is the specific, pinpointed behaviors of doing a crossword puzzle, reading a newspaper, speaking with his neighbor, and leaving the room.

We will have much more success if we focus on changing these. Learning to focus on observable behaviors will help a team develop a useful code of conduct.

EIGHT STEPS TO EFFECTIVE CONFRONTATION

The ability to confront people is one of the most critical skills a leader can possess. It's also one of the most difficult to acquire. Consider these guidelines when confronting—especially in the workplace.

1. *Confront before the problem becomes a major issue.* The potential for misunderstanding increases exponentially the longer a situation is ignored.
2. *Stick to the facts.* Don't become sidetracked in irrelevant or difficult-to-defend discussions. Focus on the behavior that needs changing, not on the individual.
3. *Be clear.* Before you meet, determine the best approach. It may be helpful to write out your thoughts and refer to your notes as necessary.
4. *Confront during a regularly scheduled meeting, if possible.* Calling a special meeting makes an individual less relaxed and therefore less prepared to deal with his or her own behavior.

5. *Get the person to agree to a change.* The goal of confrontation is to bring about a change in behavior. Reaching an agreement will focus on the issue and provide a tangible foundation should further discussion become necessary.

6. *Keep positive.* The purpose of the discussion is the individual's personal and professional development. Confrontation, when done properly, can be a very positive motivational factor.

7. *Don't accept responsibility for other people's actions.* Inevitably, as we confront issues, listeners will attempt to shift the blame. Remind them that they are responsible for their own actions, and consequences are a natural result of wrong choices.

8. *Continue to monitor the situation.* Sometimes, despite our clearest communication, we will not be able to bring people to a point of change. Be sure you have made your exceptions clear and have explained the outcome of continuing failure.[6]

RULES AND VALUES
IN RESOLVING CONFLICT

All great organizations have a core set of nonnegotiable values. We may need a whole set of them just for conflict situations. Here are some suggestions:

- We will invest time and energy together in creating win/win outcomes.
- We will attack problems and not persons. We will fix the problem, not the blame.
- We commit ourselves to listening to the other party, with the appropriate steps.
- It is never acceptable to attack a person behind his back— or even to his face.
- We will seek direct, open, and trustful communication. We absolutely will not allow conflict to be driven underground.
- It is OK to experience and express anger, fear, inadequacy, and other difficult emotions in a conflict, provided responsible restraint and mutual consideration are applied. It is

never OK to verbally or physically attack another person in a conflict.

• It is OK to have conflicts. We believe conflicts can be useful, helpful, valuable, important, and beneficial. It is not OK to keep a problem hidden or repressed.

NOTES

1. Joseph R. Cooke, *Free for the Taking* (Old Tappan, N.J.: Revell, 1975), 109–110.
2. Herbert S. Kindler, *Managing Disagreement Constructively: Conflict Management in Organizations* (Menlo Park, Calif.: Crisp, 1988), 76.
3. Ibid., 81.
4. Proverbs 25:8–9, New American Standard Bible.
5. David Augsburger, *Caring Enough to Confront* (Ventura, Calif.: Regal, 1981), 27.
6. Condensed from David Yerry, *Christian Management Report*, June 1996.

CHAPTER NINE

THE CREDIBLE COMMANDER

L eaders who want to succeed during the next decade must demonstrate credibility and trustworthiness, according to business expert James M. Kouzes. Those two qualities are the keys to successful leadership.[1] Achieving trust is no mean feat in today's cynical business climate. Lack of job security, more low-paying jobs, and fewer benefits have led to a building resentment in the workforce and a lack of faith in executives.

People don't even believe hard work is necessarily the route to success anymore. A *Newsweek* article reported that when pollsters asked how people get promoted, workers "were equally divided between how good a job one does and how politically connected one is."[2] Scott Adams, creator of Dilbert, the wildly popular cartoon that lampoons the modern workplace, takes this cynicism to the extreme: "The most ineffective workers are systematically moved to the place where they can do the least damage: management."[3]

So how do you lead people who don't believe in leaders? The answer, according to Kouzes, is to establish credibility. This, he says, is the foundation of leadership—and of all working relationships. When workers perceive management to have high credibility, they are proud to be a part of the company, see their own values as similar to those of the company, and feel a sense of ownership.

When credibility is lacking, workers produce only when watched. They are motivated primarily by money. They say good things about the company at work but actually think differently. They would leave if they could.

Kouzes identifies three components of credibility: (1) trustworthiness, (2) expertise, and (3) dynamism. We could argue that the most important of these is trustworthiness. In a huge study of what qualities people look for in leaders, the following were the most highly valued:

• Honesty (87 percent)
• Vision (forward-looking) (71 percent)
• Inspiration (66 percent)
• Competence (58 percent)[4]

WHAT IS TRUST?

Honesty, of course, is a key element of trust. What exactly is trust? We can define *trust* as an assured reliance on the character, ability, strength, and truthfulness of someone. Trust is built into a work group by promoting open communication, providing fair leadership, and supervising with sensitivity.

Trust is absolutely essential in all relationships. If I don't trust you, if I'm not sure you have my best interests at heart, there is nothing you can do that I won't regard as manipulative.

Trust is necessary to a productive working environment. It is essential for all personnel to practice open, honest communication in order to increase awareness and build cooperation. This environment of trust promotes loyalty and commitment to achieve the goals and objectives of the organization.

VALUES CREATE TRUST

In our firm, we have greatly enjoyed working with the Harley-Davidson Motor Company of Milwaukee. This high-quality company has an official list of values that are the basis of trust.

1. Tell the truth.
2. Be fair.

3. Keep your promises.
4. Respect the individual.
5. Encourage intellectual creativity.

These values are learned, memorized, and followed in this company. If all employers followed these values to the letter, cynicism would not be such a problem in the workplace. These values empower employees and are the heart of credibility.

Behaviorally, Kouzes says, credibility is practicing what you preach and doing what you say you will do. This leads to trust and motivates employees to perform. "If people perceive their leaders as more credible, they will do things more voluntarily than they will if they perceive them as not credible."[5]

CREDIBILITY IN THE WORKPLACE

Step by step, you can establish credibility in the workplace. The five-step process begins with defining the corporate culture and ends with giving good feedback.

Step 1: Define Your Corporate Culture. Help individuals clarify what they stand for, and let them know what the organization stands for. When the individual's values and the organization's values agree, you will achieve the greatest organizational commitment by the employee.

All people want to work for an organization whose mission they feel is worth giving their lives to. The authors of *Corporate Cultures*, Terrence E. Deal and Allan A. Kennedy, write, "If employees know what their company stands for, if they know what standards they are to uphold, then they are much more likely to make decisions that will support those standards. They are also more likely to feel as if they are an important part of the organization. They are motivated because life in the company has meaning for them."[6]

Step 2: Appreciate Diversity. Companies that value all their constituents are far more profitable than those that value only a few segments of their stakeholders. This includes diversity of race, ethnic origin, sex, and point of view. Show employees that you value them and their unique perspectives by getting to know them. This leads to trust.

Step 3: Affirm Shared Values. Creating wholeness from diversity is difficult but rewarding. There has to be some core of shared values. Of all the ingredients of community, this is possibly the most important. When the company and the employees share values, the employees are more personally successful, willing to work harder, longer, and smarter hours, and feel less stress.

Step 4: Empower the Employee. This step basically involves empowering employees so that they actually do something important. The Dilbert creator Adams reveals the reason for his dissatisfaction with his former position at Pacific Bell when he poignantly says, "In my seventeen-year experience, I never once did anything that helped a customer."[7]

Research indicates that employees work better when they: (1) Have latitude to meet the customer's needs; (2) have the knowledge, skill, and authority to serve the customer; and (3) are rewarded for serving the customer well.

Nearly three-quarters of workers want to derive more meaning from their work, according to a recent Gallup poll. Employees need to feel that they all serve a common purpose. One of the reasons people have become cynical today is because they view leaders as apart, distant from them. To rebuild credibility we have to become part of, not apart from, what's happening. People are more motivated when they feel a sense of ownership of the company than if they feel they're just "renting."

Kouzes speaks to this point: "Empowerment isn't just a nice thing to do, it's the right thing to do because it makes you more credible. The most controlling managers are the least believable. They project the message that they don't trust you. So you're certainly not going to trust them."[8]

In *The Empowered Manager,* Peter Block gives an excellent list of values that promote trust and empower employees. Included in the list are:

- Consistency between our plans and our actions
- Commitment to a long-term strategy
- Living out our values
- A connection between each person and the final product
- Teamwork
- A feeling of value and respect in each person
- Meaningful work
- Control of our own destiny

- Partnership with each other
- Each person expressing real feelings and staying engaged in the mission[9]

The empowered manager creates a workplace where people want to work by using what are called the VIP motivators: validation, information, and participation.

Validation involves respecting employees as people, being flexible to meet their personal needs, and encouraging them to learn, grow, and develop new skills.

Information means keeping employees abreast of what's going on in the company.

Participation involves giving employees control over how they do their work and input on decisions that affect them.

These motivators succeed because employees are more likely to help you get a job done if they feel they are treated as adults, that the company will consider their needs, that they know why they are doing things, and that they get to help decide the best way to fulfill the company's goals.[10]

The empowered manager helps employees be the best by creating a climate that encourages self-development. This means providing:

- A basic understanding of the employee's job and its contribution to the team
- A continuing understanding of what is expected
- The opportunity to participate in planning change and to perform in keeping with ability
- Assistance when needed
- Feedback on how well the employee is doing

Step 5: Give Good Feedback. Giving feedback can be dicey. When people are criticized, they tend to get angry and feel stress. They avoid the person they expect will criticize them and often withhold information (especially bad news) and creative ideas. They also tend to make more mistakes.

When not given correctly, feedback simply becomes criticism. That can lead the employee to feel that either he or you are no good. He doesn't hear the specific problems you're having—

all he knows is he has failed. The usual response is to feel he's no good. The employee becomes defensive and thinks you're just out to get him. In either case, the criticism is destructive rather than constructive.

Let's remember what real feedback is: information on an employee's performance or behavior given in such a way that the person knows exactly what to do to change or improve.

Feedback is nonjudgmental, descriptive, and tactful. It focuses on the behavior rather than on the person. Feedback is specific rather than general and is directed toward behavior that is under that person's control and can be changed. Good feedback focuses on the value it may have to the employee, not on the "release" it provides for the manager.

Positive feedback involves valuing and accepting employees, showing faith so that they come to believe in themselves. When you give positive feedback, you recognize efforts and improvement (rather than requiring a fixed numerical level of achievement) and show appreciation for contributions.

When giving feedback, follow these guidelines:

- Get the receiver's permission first. "Are you open to some feedback?"
- Give feedback at appropriate times, the more immediate the better.
- Make feedback tentative, not absolute. Get the person's input.
- Check with the receiver for clear understanding.

Positive feedback is essential when employees approach a manager with an idea. How the manager responds can determine whether the employee continues sharing ideas in the future. As we discussed above, destructive criticism can lead employees to withhold ideas. When an employee approaches you with a creative idea, follow these idea-building guidelines:

- Validate the other person's idea before adding your response.
- Avoid blanket disagreements.
- Don't discount the person offering the idea.

- Use "and" to connect your thoughts rather than "but" or "however."
- Build on the idea by adding what you like.

TREAT THEM BETTER THAN THEY ARE

Empowered managers help employees develop their full potential by treating them as if they had already achieved it. Goethe said, "If you treat an individual as he is, he will stay that way, but if you treat him as if he were what he could be, he will become what he could be."

Jesus was a prime example of an empowering manager. He treated people according to what they had the capacity to become. Although Peter was a hot-tempered, unreliable disciple, Jesus saw his potential stability and told him, "I tell you that you are Peter the rock, and it is on this rock that I am going to found my Church."[11] Jesus' words became a self-fulfilling prophecy—within a few years, Peter had played a commanding role in building Christ's new community in the world.

Whether consciously or unconsciously, a leader often projects his own strengths and weaknesses onto his subjects, says Parker J. Palmer:

> A leader is a person who has an unusual degree of power to project on other people his or her shadow, or his or her light. A leader is a person who has an unusual degree of power to create the conditions under which other people must live and move and have their being—conditions that can either be as illuminating as heaven or as shadowy as hell. A leader is a person who must take special responsibility for what's going on inside him or her self, inside his or her consciousness, lest the act of leadership create more harm than good.[12]

In order to project light rather than shadow, Palmer says, a leader must develop spiritual insight into himself and overcome five shadows:

- Insecurity about his own worth. Leaders manifest this shadow by creating settings in which other people are deprived of their identities.
- The perception that life is a competition. This becomes a self-fulfilling prophecy, leading to fiercer competition.

- The belief that he is ultimately responsible for everything (called "functional atheism"). This leads to workaholism, stress, strained relationships, and unhealthy priorities.
- Fear of ambiguity. The leader projects this shadow by implementing rigid rules and procedures, leading to corporate cultures that are imprisoning rather than empowering.
- Denial of death. This leads to maintaining projects and programs that are outdated and no longer useful rather than changing with the times.

Palmer is absolutely convinced that only spiritually based leaders can survive, because only the person whose life is built on faith knows:

- Who he is doesn't depend on his position or professional title.
- There is harmony in the universe.
- All the responsibility isn't on his shoulders—it's okay to ask for help.
- Chaos is necessary for creativity.
- Death leads to new life—we learn from our failures.[13]

THE VOICE AND THE TOUCH

Max DePree is the gifted chairman of the Herman Miller Company, one of the primary innovators in the furniture business for sixty years and regularly included in *Fortune* magazine's list of the most admired American companies. He was recently elected to the National Business Hall of Fame. In his latest book, he tells this moving personal story:

> Esther, my wife, and I have a granddaughter named Zoe, the Greek word for "life." She was born prematurely and weighed one pound, seven ounces, so small that my wedding ring could slide up her arm to her shoulder. The neonatologist who first examined her told us that she had a 5 to 10 percent chance of living three days. When Esther and I scrubbed up for our first visit and saw Zoe in her isolette in the neonatal intensive care unit, she had two IV's in her navel, one in her foot, a monitor in each side of her chest, and a respirator tube and a feeding tube in her mouth.
>
> To complicate matters, Zoe's biological father had jumped ship the month before Zoe was born. Realizing this, a wise and caring nurse named Ruth gave me my instructions. "For the next several

months you are the surrogate father. I want you to come to the hospital every day to visit Zoe, and when you come, I would like you to rub her body and her legs and arms with the tip of your finger. While you're caressing her, you should tell her over and over how much you love her, how glad you are she's in the world and how proud you are of her."[14]

One day Max and Esther asked Ruth why it was so important to continue talking while they stroked Zoe. Nurse Ruth explained this was essential so the infant could connect the voice and the touch. When this infant, clinging to life, knew that the voice and the touch were the same, she would know that these were people she could trust. These were people she could respond to and come alive under.

Max comments that Nurse Ruth had given him the best possible definition of authentic leadership. When the voice and the touch are the same in a leader, people can relax, be themselves, grow, admit their own failures and inadequacies, seek forgiveness and renewal, and come alive (as now beautiful, lively four-year-old Zoe did).

I once knew a leader who was brilliant, skilled, articulate, and talented. The problem was that the person who spoke from the platform and the person you encountered in real life were totally different. The voice and the touch were just never the same. Eventually, everyone lost faith in him. He forfeited his right to lead.

Leaders who walk the talk, practice what they preach, and live what they espouse are desperately needed in today's world. They won't be perfect, but you'll always know the voice and the touch are the same.

NOTES

1. James M. Kouzes, *The Credibility Factor: Why Constituents Demand It, How Leaders Earn It*, video, (Stanford University Media Group, 1993).
2. Steven Levy, "Working in Dilbert's World," *Newsweek*, 12 August 1996, 56.
3. Ibid., 54.
4. Kouzes, *The Credibility Factor.*
5. Ibid.
6. Terrence E. Deal and Allan A. Kennedy, *Corporate Cultures*, (Reading, Mass.: Addison Wesley, 1982), 186.
7. Steven Levy, "Strip Mining the Corporate Life," *Newsweek*, 12 August 1996, 54.
8. Kouzes, *The Credibility Factor.*
9. Peter Block, *The Empowered Manager* (San Francisco: Jossey Bass, 1987), 114.
10. Ibid., 115.

11. Matthew 16:18, J. B. Phillips, trans., *The New Testament in Modern English* (New York: Macmillan, 1958), 36.
12. Parker J. Palmer, *Leading From Within: Reflections on Spirituality and Leadership* (Indiana Office for Campus Ministries, 1990), 5.
13. Ibid., 11–16.
14. Max DePree, *Leadership Jazz: The Art of Conducting Business* (New York: Dell, 1992), Prologue.

A PREEMPTIVE STRIKE FOR PEACE

CHAPTER TEN

AWAKENING TO WHAT REALLY MATTERS

A cartoon in the July 1996 issue of *Training* showed a group of businesspeople sitting around a conference table looking grim, except for the chairman of the group, who was determinedly pounding his fist. A chart on the wall showed a once-rising line now plummeting downward. The chairman was saying, "I say we hang the darned thing upside down and go home!"

How very appropriate for today's world. Our approach to problems is quite often to deny, to alter the data rather than face the music and work toward a solution. We all have "belief filters" —screening mechanisms through which we process life's little curveballs.

To reduce the destructive conflict in organizations we must lay aside our filters and passivity. We must attack. We must proactively pursue the following strategies.

FOCUS ON THE CUSTOMER

Once I was called in to help mediate a terrible employee relations atmosphere in a large corporation. The mood was totally adversarial. I've never seen such misunderstanding, distrust, and hatred between two groups.

Just to give you an idea . . . although the union contract required members to attend my meetings on team building and reconciliation, it did not specify which way the chairs were to face. I had the unique experience of walking into a room full of workers with half of them looking the other way!

One day I asked a group of production workers how many had ever talked directly to a customer. Not a single hand went up.

So we abandoned the useless meetings and began to send out teams of managers and workers to the marketplace. They visited dealerships, stores, and end users. Workers began to see why quality problems were causing them to lose market share. Managers began to see how their unresponsive bureaucracy was creating problems for their customers as well as their workers.

On the bus heading back, they began to talk to each other about how to fix these problems. The whole atmosphere began to change. They began to see each other as resources, not enemies. They began to understand that:

• Everything does not begin and end with management;
• Everything does not begin and end with workers;
• Everything does begin and end with the customer.

Do you want to lessen conflict in your organization? My strongest recommendation is to focus everyone's attention on the customer.

ARTICULATE YOUR CORPORATE VALUES

Your corporate values should be clear to every employee. A leading health care company articulates the following values:

Quality: We welcome our customers' high expectations. We constantly strive to meet and exceed those expectations. These high standards will make us recognized in the communities we serve, as well as nationally, for the excellence of our staff, our programs, and our therapy.

Integrity: We conduct ourselves in an open, honest, ethical manner. We understand and respect the privacy and dignity of the individuals we serve.

Financial Accountability: Everyone is rewarded when we deliver quality care in financially responsible ways. Each of our people is expected to be a sound decision maker with a commitment to our customers' high productivity requirements.

Teamwork and Pleasant Work Environment: We are committed to being the employer of choice for the top talent in our industry. We will be a force working together in harmony, challenged by new opportunities, supported by our work environment, and guided by our Core Values.

A leading auto insurance company articulates these values:

Integrity: We revere honesty. We adhere to high ethical standards, report completely, encourage disclosing bad news and welcome disagreement.

Golden Rule: We respect all people, value the differences among them and deal with them in the way we want to be dealt with. This requires us to know ourselves and to try to understand others.

Objectives: We strive to be clear and open about the Company's ambitious objectives and our people's personal and team objectives. We evaluate performance against all these objectives.

Excellence: We strive constantly to improve in order to meet and exceed the highest expectations of our customers, shareholders and people. "Quality" is our process for teaching and encouraging our people to improve performance and reduce costs of what they do for customers. We base reward on results and promotion on ability.

Profit: The free enterprise system rewards most those who most enhance the health and happiness of their customers, communities and people. Profit motivates the Company to invest in new ways to do this. Enhancing people's health and happiness is the ultimate goal, and healthy, happy people do it best.

What organization would not lessen the toxic type of anger and conflict by training its people in these values, these expressions of integrity?

In selecting leaders, emphasize values and character as well as credentials. Joseph Stowell reminds us:

Credentials are transient; character is permanent. Credentials build memories about what we have done; character builds a legacy for others to follow. Credentials are locked into one person; character is transferable. Credentials will get us in the front door; character will keep us there. Credentials tend to evoke jealousy; character attracts respect and stimulates others to develop character as well.

Character commits itself to principle over personal gain. To people over things. To servanthood over lordship. To the long view over the immediate.[1]

SET BENCHMARKS FOR EXCELLENCE

Settle for nothing less than excellence in the organization—right down to the details.

John Gardner, in his book *Excellence*, says, "The society which scorns excellence in plumbing because plumbing is a humble activity, and tolerates shoddiness in philosophy because it is an exalted activity, will have neither good plumbing nor good philosophy. Neither its pipes nor its theories will hold water."[2]

CULTIVATE A CULTURE OF TRUST

Trust is an assured reliance on the character, ability, and strength or truth of someone or something. Establishing trust in a work group requires open and honest communication, accepting others, sharing a common goal, and respecting the opinions of others on how to achieve that goal. The result of greater trust is greater productivity.

DRAW ON RESOURCES OUTSIDE YOURSELF

In the Scriptures, the apostle Paul set an unusual standard for leaders:

Do nothing from selfishness or empty conceit, but with humility of mind let each of you regard one another as more important than himself; do not merely look out for your own personal interests, but also for the interests of others. Have this attitude in yourselves which was also in Christ Jesus, who, although He existed in the form of God, did not regard equality with God a thing to be grasped, but emptied Himself, taking the form of a bond-servant, and being made in the likeness of men. And being found in appearance as a man, He humbled Himself by becoming obedient to the point of death, even death on a cross.[3]

For me, personally, this is the mental and emotional point to which I must finally come in order to stay calm about my most severe conflicts. I must arrive at the place of humility. Whose offense toward me has been so outrageous that I cannot move beyond it?

Once I begin to think this way, I begin to see Sherman Tanks and Stealthy Stalkers in a new light. I don't see just their posturing, their pettiness, their politics; I see the person, the supremely valuable and important person.

I love Dr. Oliver Sacks' remarkable book *Awakenings*, in which he tells the story of two miracles. In 1969, a number of hopeless post-encephalitic patients in a small hospital in a New York suburb were given the drug L–dopa. One of these patients was Leonard, a man "in his forty–sixth year, completely speechless and completely without voluntary motion except for minute movements of the right hand. With these he could spell out messages on a small letter board—this had been his only mode of communication for fifteen years."[4]

In the film version we see Leonard with his mouth hanging open, his head torqued to one side, his hands curled in a grotesque manner. Hospitalized since his youth, Leonard is given large amounts of L–dopa by his doctor . . . and Leonard comes alive. He walks and talks much like a healthy human being.

Sacks writes, "He was like a man who had awoken from a nightmare of a serious illness, or a man released from entombment or prison, who is suddenly intoxicated with the sense and beauty of everything round him."[5]

The change is so amazing that the hospital staff collects enough money to administer the same massive and costly doses of L–dopa to a large number of similar patients. One by one these people improve markedly and become almost normal, each manifesting a unique and delightful personality.

But meanwhile, something unforeseen is happening. Leonard is beginning to show side effects. They're sad to behold—violent ticks and jerks that rack his body. The doctors begin to realize that the awakening was just for a short period of time. First Leonard, and then all the others, will soon go back to their former state.

So the story is wonderful and also terribly sad. But then a second miracle occurs.

Before the awakenings, the hospital staff had viewed these pitiful people as just a part of their job—creatures to feed or to clean up again and again. Now the patients had become unique individuals trapped by a terrible disease inside the prison of their own bodies.

The staff came to understand more fully that these patients must be treated with dignity and love. In the months ahead, the nurses and others would read to them, comb their hair, and go the extra mile to make sure they were as comfortable as possible.

Many people read this book (or see the film) and miss the whole point. The greater awakening is not with the patients but with the staff—an awakening of the heart, the inner spirit. While the first awakening was temporary, the second was permanent.

POWER FOR THE TASKS

Phillips Brooks was a distinguished preacher in the late 1800s and the author of the well-known Christmas carol "O Little Town of Bethlehem." He was also a man who suffered from deep periods of self-doubt and melancholia. Among his papers after his death were found these words:

> O God, we do not pray for easy lives.
> We do not pray for tasks equal to powers.
> We pray rather for a power to come and live within us
> That will make us equal to our tasks.
> For then the doing of our daily work will be no miracle.
> Rather, something far more wonderful will occur—
> We will be a miracle!

Despite his struggles, Brooks knew that his prayer was an actual possibility. People really could live this way—with poise and confidence and peace, even amid threats and problems. It is an apt prayer for leaders and managers today, more than a hundred years after it was written. We are dealing with more than cantankerous people. We are dealing with the potential for miracles.

NOTES

1. Joseph Stowell, "Credentials or Character?" *Moody*, November 1996, 4.
2. John W. Gardner, *Excellence* (New York: Norton, 1995).
3. Philippians 2:3–8, New American Standard Bible.
4. Oliver Sacks, *Awakenings* (New York: Harper Collins, 1973), 203.
5. Ibid., 200.

If you are interested in information
about other books written from a
biblical perspective, please write
to the following address:

Northfield Publishing
215 West Locust Street
Chicago, IL 60610